LEADING
Through
Quality
Questioning

Creating Capacity, Commitment, and Community

JACKIE ACREE WALSH
BETH DANKERT SATTES

CORWIN
A SAGE Company

For information:

Corwin
A SAGE Company
2455 Teller Road
Thousand Oaks, California 91320
(800) 233-9936
Fax: (800) 417-2466
www.corwin.com

SAGE Pvt. Ltd.
B 1/I 1 Mohan Cooperative
    Industrial Area
Mathura Road, New Delhi 110 044
India

SAGE Ltd.
1 Oliver's Yard
55 City Road
London EC1Y 1SP
United Kingdom

SAGE Asia-Pacific Pte. Ltd.
33 Pekin Street #02-01
Far East Square
Singapore 048763

Printed in the United States of America

Library of Congress Cataloging-in-Publication Data

Walsh, Jackie A.
Leading through quality questioning : creating capacity, commitment, and community / Jackie Acree Walsh and Beth Dankert Sattes.
    p. cm.
Includes bibliographical references and index.
ISBN 978-1-4129-6061-8 (pbk.)
    1. Questioning. 2. Thought and thinking. I. Sattes, Beth D. (Beth Dankert) II. Title.

LB1027.44.W33 2010
371.3'7—dc22   2009047365

This book is printed on acid-free paper.

11   12   13   14   10   9   8   7   6   5   4   3

Acquisitions Editor:	Hudson Perigo
Associate Editor:	Julie McNall
Editorial Assistants:	Brett Ory and Allison Scott
Production Editor:	Veronica Stapleton
Copy Editor:	Adam Dunham
Typesetter:	C&M Digitals (P) Ltd.
Proofreader:	Dennis W. Webb
Indexer:	Molly Hall
Cover Designer:	Michael Dubowe

LEADING
Through
Quality
Questioning

In memory of our fathers, Jack K. Acree and Herbert W. H. Dankert,
whose lives were our best lessons in leadership

Contents

1. **Quality Questioning: Why Is This an Important Practice
   for Leaders of Learning Communities?**

   The opening chapter makes the argument that quality questioning is a
   key skill for transformational leaders who wish to engage all members
   of their community in learning and change. This rationale draws from
   research, theory, and best practice. Included is the organizer for the
   remainder of the book, the Leading Through Quality Questioning
   (LQQ) Framework, which is a two-dimensional matrix that highlights
   four elements of quality questioning and four leadership functions.

2. **Questioning as a Process: What Are the Essential Elements?**

   This chapter explicates the questioning dimension of the Leading
   Through Quality Questioning Framework by offering research and
   best practices associated with its four elements: (1) framing or crafting
   a question, (2) presenting the question effectively, (3) extending thinking through a variety of verbal and nonverbal prompts, and (4) encouraging a schoolwide culture of inquiry in which "not knowing" is
   valued and questions are welcomed. Among the resources offered
   within the chapter are examples of quality questions and stems for use
   in promoting thinking.

In this chapter, we associate the leadership function of *maximizing* with the development of individual and organizational potential or capacity. After highlighting research findings, we offer a mental model for leader reflection and a scenario featuring one principal's work to develop individual and collective efficacy and to nurture an "it's our job" approach to teaching all students well.

This chapter defines *mobilizing* as moving individuals and groups to action. We showcase quality questioning as a process that enables leaders to build ownership and commitment across a community. A scenario illustrates how to nurture dialogue by combining quality questions with protocols for group response. Also featured is a tool for use in developing behaviors that are critical to dialogue.

The point of view presented in this chapter is that *mediating* in a learning organization is about helping individuals understand different perspectives and find common ground by focusing on shared purpose. Leaders who seek to follow this path require new frames for thinking about conflict as well as renewed skills and tools that support their work in this area. Two scenarios embody suggested frames, principles, skills, and tools.

Emphasizing the value of self-assessment and self-monitoring, this chapter demonstrates the connection between formulating relevant and appropriate questions and implementing effective progress monitoring. Included are examples of monitoring both classroom and schoolwide programs and initiatives.

The final chapter focuses on what leaders can do to model and encourage quality questioning in others. A scenario chronicles the case of a principal who is committed to nurturing a culture of questioning and inquiry in her school. The chapter refers readers to Resource C, a self-assessment that leaders can use to determine their Quality Questioning Quotient.

List of Tables and Figures

Preface

What Have We Learned From Our Work? Quality Questioning Is Not Just for the Classroom Anymore

FOCUS QUESTIONS

1. Why is it important for school leaders to embrace quality questioning?

2. What is meant by *quality questioning*?

3. Which leadership functions can quality questioning most effectively support?

4. What is the organization of this book?

Over the past two decades, we have been working with teachers and school leaders to improve classroom questioning practices to increase student learning. In *Quality Questioning: Research-Based Practice to Engage Every Learner* (Walsh & Sattes, 2005), we acknowledged an important learning from our work: *If classroom questioning practices are to improve and produce desired outcomes, both teachers and students must understand and use quality questioning.* This was a refinement of our earlier thinking, which focused primarily on improving teacher practice. We now propose a further refinement: *If quality questioning is to flourish in the classrooms of a school, it must be embraced by teachers, students, and school leaders.* When teachers and school staff operate within a professional community of inquiry, they are better able to support and sustain inquiry-oriented classrooms.

A diverse set of experiences brought us to this conclusion. First, conversations with leaders in schools that had adopted quality questioning as a focus for classroom improvement provided anecdotal evidence: In schools where leaders assumed an inquiry-oriented approach to planning and decision making, teachers were more successful in implementing and sustaining improved questioning practices with and for students. Second, Jackie's work with school improvement and instructional coaches demonstrated the value of questioning in the facilitation of adult learning and growth in schools. Third, our collaboration in the development of a statewide training and support system for the mentors of new teachers underscored the value of quality questions and questioning in supporting the development of neophytes to the profession. Finally, our training and consulting with school and district leaders about school culture affirmed our belief in the power of questioning and dialogue to nurture and sustain change. These experiences, and our reflection on them, served as inspiration and fodder for this book.

What Do We Mean by *Quality Questioning?*

Quality questioning is a process for engaging individuals in thinking together. It begins with the crafting of a focused, purposeful, engaging question and continues with the intentional use of strategies that facilitate and sustain thinking. This process can thrive only in a culture of inquiry that is supported by shared norms and habits of mind. Quality questioning is useful in classrooms, schools, and other venues where individuals come together to learn and create.

Which Leadership Functions Are Most Enhanced by Quality Questioning?

Quality questioning practices enhance the ongoing informal and formal communications in which leaders engage—regardless of the purpose or context for the communication. However, certain leadership functions are particularly supported by quality questioning. We spotlight four of these functions in this book: maximizing, mobilizing, mediating, and monitoring. When coupled with quality questioning, the execution of these functions takes a school leader beyond management and into the realm of true leadership. We define these functions as follows:

- *Maximizing* relates to the development of individual and organizational potential and capacity.
- *Mobilizing* is the process of getting folks on board, motivated, and committed to attaining an organization's vision or goals.

- *Mediating* refers to the means by which leaders help create common ground between and among members of their community.
- *Monitoring* engages individuals in assessing the extent to which they are progressing individually and collectively toward identified benchmarks.

We view leadership expansively, as a practice, not a position; hence, each of the above functions can be performed by leaders at all levels within the educational environment—from the school superintendent to the school principal to the classroom teacher to the student. The scenarios in this book, however, feature school and district leaders.

What Is the Organization of *Leading Through Quality Questioning?*

We designed this book as a hands-on manual of practice for education leaders at all levels. While readers need not proceed sequentially from Chapters 1 to 7, we suggest that you begin with Chapters 1 and 2. In Chapter 1, we present the Leading Through Quality Questioning Framework and a rationale for adopting this approach; in Chapter 2, we elaborate on the questioning skills and strategies associated with this practice.

Chapters 3 through 6 focus on the four leadership functions: maximizing, mobilizing, mediating, and monitoring. These chapters can be read in any order, depending upon the reader's interest. Each features one or more scenarios based on real cases or composites; the names of schools and individuals, however, are fictional. Throughout these chapters, we highlight various structured group processes that leaders have used to engage members of a school community in thinking and responding together. Detailed instructions for facilitating 20 of these processes are included in Resource B. The success of each process depends upon the formulation of quality questions to drive the conversation. We have used each of these processes countless times to engage educators in quality conversations. We invite you to experiment with them as you seek to expand and enrich inquiry across your community.

The scenario in Chapter 7 features a principal who is a composite of several principals with whom we have worked. This school leader is struggling with how to transform her school into an inquiry-centered school in which quality questioning characterizes adult and student interactions. While there is no single how-to or simple formula for building such a community, this scenario profiles one approach. The chapter references a self-assessment, the Quality Questioning Quotient, which is included as Resource C. We hope you will use this self-assessment individually and with your staff as a tool for reflection and professional growth.

Quality questioning is a dynamic that is best learned experientially. We were challenged to reduce this dynamic to words on a page. It is our hope that readers will try out strategies, experiment with sample questions, and reflect on their experiences. We hope, too, that you will share these experiences with us, and contact us when we can support your learning.

Acknowledgments

Enhanced insights and learnings emerge from reflection and dialogue. Over the 20-plus years of our work together, we have engaged in dialogue with hundreds of clients and colleagues about the practice and potential of quality questioning. Their insights and questions were catalysts for our deeper reflection about the implications of quality questioning for educators in varying contexts. Their stories were inspirations for the scenarios presented in this book. While we cannot mention each one of these individually, we are deeply appreciative for their interest and support.

We single out the following individuals without whose influence we would not have completed this project. Betty Burks, Deputy Superintendent for Curriculum and Instruction, San Antonio Independent School District, first encouraged us to expand our work in quality questioning to the leadership arena. Tony Thacker, Coordinator of the Alabama Governor's Commission on Quality Teaching, shared deeply from his personal experience as principal of an alternative high school and motivated us to continue our endeavor when we were stalled. Cathy Gassenheimer, Director of the Alabama Best Practices Center, made it possible for Jackie to work with and learn from leaders at all levels across the state. Carla McClure, a long-time friend and colleague, read the manuscript multiple times and provided critical-friend feedback. Hudson Perigo, Executive Editor at Corwin, was patient, encouraging, and supportive over the course of the project.

Finally, we acknowledge the ongoing love and support provided by our families who have enabled us to blend our professional endeavors into our lives as wives and mothers.

About the Authors

Jackie Acree Walsh, PhD, and **Beth Dankert Sattes** are long-time advocates of quality questioning for students, teachers, and school leaders. Authors of *Quality Questioning: Research-Based Practice to Engage Every Learner* (Corwin, 2005), they have provided professional development in classroom questioning for thousands of teachers and school leaders in more than 30 states. They are codevelopers of *Questioning and Understanding to Improve Learning and Thinking* (QUILT), a nationally validated professional development program on effective questioning and copresenters of the Video Journal in Education series *Questioning to Stimulate Thinking* (1999). Included in their other joint endeavors are the creation of professional development modules on improving school culture (for the Southern Regional Education Board) and leading learning communities (for the Alabama Leadership Academy).

 **Jackie Acree Walsh** holds a bachelor's degree in political science from Duke University, a master's degree in teaching (MAT) from the University of North Carolina at Chapel Hill, and a PhD in educational administration and supervision from the University of Alabama. Beginning her career as a high school social studies teacher, she has worked in university administration, at a state department of education, and as a research and development specialist at a regional educational laboratory. In recent years, she has worked as an independent consultant, specializing in design and facilitation of learning experiences for adults with an emphasis upon questioning, classroom coaching, and leadership. Jackie can be reached at WalshJA@aol.com.

Beth Dankert Sattes holds a bachelor's degree from Vanderbilt University and a master's degree in early childhood special education from Peabody College. A former teacher, she worked in research and development at Edvantia (formerly AEL, a regional educational laboratory) in professional development and in parent and community partnerships with schools. Currently, she heads Enthused Learning, an educational consulting company. Beth can be reached at Beth@EnthusedLearning.com.

1

Quality Questioning

Why Is This an Important Practice for Leaders of Learning Communities?

Questions require discipline in asking them, a discipline we seldom practice. No matter how simple the questions, we most often rush past them. We feel compelled to act rather than inquire.

—Myron Rogers, "Bringing Life to Organizational Change"

FOCUS QUESTIONS

1. Why is quality questioning an essential skill for today's education leaders?

2. What are the essential elements of the quality questioning process?

3. What is the relationship between quality questioning and leadership functions that support high-performance learning communities?

The *whos* and the *whats* of school leadership are strikingly different today than in decades past. Contemporary leadership embraces individuals serving in a variety of new roles and discharging a wide range of responsibilities, many of which were not in play a generation ago. In fact, the terminology that describes many current roles and responsibilities is itself relatively new. For example, the following descriptions, commonplace today, would have had many educators scratching their heads not long ago.

> *A school principal seeks to maximize the potential of all members of the school community by encouraging them to assume an "it's my job" approach to teaching all students.*

> *An assistant superintendent for instruction creates a district learning collaborative to mobilize leaders around a shared vision for teaching and learning in a culture of change.*

> *A school principal mediates a conflict between a parent and a beginning teacher through the use of dialogue.*

> *A school principal helps a faculty come to a shared understanding of the purpose and procedures of assigning grades to students.*

> *A literacy coach collaborates with a team of teachers to monitor their implementation of new teaching strategies.*

> *In solving an attendance problem, a school faculty creates new strategies for monitoring programs and practices.*

These statements describe but a few of the challenges confronting contemporary school leaders. As these leaders address critical issues, the following three truths become self-evident:

1. *There are no ready-made, simple, fail-proof solutions.* As a result, the capacity of a leader to formulate incisive questions is a more important skill than the ability to advocate for one particular solution or answer.

2. *Even if there were a surefire solution, the changes demanded of the individuals required to do the work cannot be mandated.* Hence, the

ability of a leader to engage others in reflection and dialogue that help individuals find personal meaning in proposed changes is more desirable than charisma, which might elicit only temporary compliance.

3. *And even if such changes could be mandated, the results would be ephemeral at best if the individuals and organization did not concurrently develop the capacity to monitor and adjust, given the constancy of change in our global society.* Therefore, the leader who nurtures a culture in which individuals routinely inquire into the impact of their behaviors and activities is far more effective than the leader who monitors with a heavy hand.

Effective leadership in these challenging and complex times depends, to an increasing extent, on the skillful use of quality questioning. It's that simple—and that complex.

How Is the Context Changing for Leaders?

Many school leaders are redefining educational leadership as they seek to cope with the sometimes-conflicting challenges of test-based accountability and the preparation of students for an uncertain future. School leadership is being transformed by interconnected patterns related to the following three cultural shifts in education.

1. From command-and-control decision making in a bureaucratic organization to the sharing of leadership across the learning community

2. From a right-answer orientation to a culture of inquiry

3. From individual autonomy to collective responsibility for the learning of all

Within this context, effective leadership depends on mastery of quality questioning's essential elements.

The traditional, bureaucratic structure of schools features a top-down, command-and-control governance system—from the superintendent's office to school principals, from the principal's office to classroom teachers, and from the teacher's desk to students. Compliance is an expected outcome of an effective command-and-control system.

The familiar lines from Alfred Lord Tennyson's (2005–2009/1854) *The Charge of the Light Brigade* comes to mind: "Theirs not to make reply, / Theirs not to reason why, / Theirs but to do and die." In such a system, leaders typically make decisions and pass them down the line of subordinates; they do not pose questions or encourage thinking and discourse concerning alternative approaches. Although widely recognized as an outmoded paradigm for leadership, vestiges of this mode are alive and well in many quarters. However, advocates for learning organizations challenge the premises on which command-and-control leadership rests.

Engaging people throughout an organization or school community in meaningful conversations is the defining characteristic of learning organizations, learning communities, and professional learning communities—concepts that have dominated professional literature over the past two decades. With the publication of *The Fifth Discipline* in 1990, Peter Senge popularized the concept of *learning organizations* that demanded increased collaborative inquiry within organizations. Senge and others argue that learning organizations promote the efficiency and effectiveness of individuals at all levels of an organization by engaging them in inquiry and accompanying learning. Senge, Kleiner, Roberts, Ross, and Smith (1994) define inquiry as "holding conversations where we openly share views and develop knowledge about each other's assumptions" (p. 237). They further offer a set of tools and skills that we can draw upon as we seek to become better practitioners of inquiry.

The formulation of powerful questions is at the heart of productive inquiry. The right questions, however, are only catalysts for successful inquiry. If the inquiry is to produce useful results, it must be situated in a culture where individuals value active listening, demonstrate respect toward one another, and are willing to suspend judgment when conflicting points of view emerge. Additionally, individuals need skills in discussion and dialogue—skills that are associated with quality questioning.

Harvard Professor David Perkins (2003) calls for inquiry-centered leaders to nurture this type of culture. He contrasts inquiry-centered leadership to answer-centered leadership, in which leaders "declare what's to be done and why":

> An inquiry-centered leader . . . would encourage others' questions, facilitate conversations, initiate investigations, welcome multiple viewpoints, and the like. Inquiry-centered leaders let others do a lot of the thinking and let them take credit for it.
>
> Beyond direct personal contact, an inquiry-centered leader fosters organizational structures that support inquiry—for instance,

small teams composed of diverse expertise, matrix structures that promote organizational crosstalk, or support for small-scale testing of risky innovations with high potential. (p. 99)

In Perkins's view, answer-centered leadership suffers from at least three limitations. It does not "address strongly the leadership goal of motivation," nor does it "promote the individual or collective growth of the participants, who become dependent upon the leader." Additionally, "the leader, who is supposed to have the answers, may have none, or not good enough ones" (p. 97). Clearly, inquiry-centered leaders situate themselves in a learning organization or community. In a learning community, both the leader and the constituents move away from the quest for an immediate "right answer" to the framing of important challenges and problems. They embrace the belief that they must first seek out the right questions.

The tendency to seek right answers or quick fixes is one of the impediments to the development of a culture of inquiry. The well-known maxim "Ready, *fire*, aim" conveys the compulsion of many to act, rather than inquire. In today's complex, rapidly changing context, leaders run the risk of adopting superficial, short-lived solutions when they rush to action without considering what is really worth doing (Block, 2003). Current thought leaders argue strongly for bringing members of a community together to grapple with important questions—to engage in inquiry before action (Block, 2003; Johnson, 2005; Lambert, 2002). Among the difficulties inherent in quick fixes are (1) the tendency to adopt solutions that are not consistent or congruent with an organization's deeper purposes and (2) the failure to engage the people responsible for implementation in conversations about the *what* and the *why* of the change. Failure to help people understand the meaning of changes usually results in little buy-in or ownership. When this happens, both quality and sustainability are compromised.

Most human beings, especially well-educated ones, buy into something only after they have had a chance to wrestle with it. Wrestling means asking questions, challenging, and arguing.

—John Kotter (1996, pp. 99–100)

The construction of meaning is a theme that runs throughout the work of Michael Fullan, one of today's leading researchers in educational change and leadership. Fullan (2007) posits that "a core question for educational practitioners is how to combine 'meaning' and 'action' to achieve continuous improvement on a sustainable scale never before experienced" (p. xii). He reports that, too often, change is introduced to schools without the "opportunity for teachers to engage in deeper questioning and sustained learning" about the what and why of the change. "As a result, meaningful reform escapes the typical teacher, in favor of superficial, episodic reform that makes matters worse" (p. 28). This superficial, episodic reform is the result of action without inquiry, the problem referenced in the quote from Myron Rogers at the beginning of this chapter.

Bypassing dialogue about the nature of a problem, issue, or challenge can lead to another trap: failure to distinguish between technical problems and adaptive or generative problems. Fullan (2005) describes technical challenges as those that can be addressed with existing knowledge and/or technology.

> A technical problem would be teaching a child to read or raising literacy proficiency scores from 57% to 75%, as was the case in England. Not that technical problems are easy to solve, but we do know how to approach them. An adaptive challenge is one for which we do not have the answers. Engaging alienated or unmotivated students, involving parents and the community at large, addressing social inclusion of special needs students, moving from 75% to 90% literacy, and reforming high schools are all examples of current adaptive problems. (p. 53)

Fullan and others suggest that a key to addressing adaptive problems is to pose the right kinds of questions for dialogue to those who know the problem up close and personal.

What Is the Framework for Leading Through Quality Questioning?

Leaders seeking to develop the skills and dispositions associated with quality questioning can benefit from a framework that organizes research and theory about questioning and leadership. In an earlier book (2005), we developed a framework for quality questioning for classroom use. School leaders reported finding components of the framework useful in engaging adults in conversations related to problems and issues. These reports, along with requests for additional information, led to the formulation of the *Leading Through Quality Questioning (LQQ) Framework* (Figure 1.1).

| Figure 1.1 | The Leading Through Quality Questioning (LQQ) Framework |

Elements of Quality Questioning	Leadership Functions			
	Maximizing	Mobilizing	Mediating	Monitoring
Crafting Quality Questions				
Presenting Questions to Engage All				
Extending Thinking				
Creating a Culture of Inquiry				

The LQQ Framework is two dimensional. The first dimension is related to the four elements of quality questioning that inquiry-centered leaders understand and use.

1. *Crafting Quality Questions* refers to the formulation of questions that are purposeful, clearly focused, and understandable. This requires consideration of the kind of information being sought as well as the context in which it will be used.

2. *Presenting Questions to Encourage Engagement* underscores the importance of thinking about *how* individuals will be engaged in responding to questions. This element reminds us of the value of listening to a wide range of voices—not just the usual, more vocal members of our community. To achieve this, we need to know and use a wide range of processes and strategies that structure and facilitate involvement.

3. *Extending Thinking* involves the intentional use of strategies that encourage and support deep thinking. For example, "wait times" (pauses of 3 to 5 seconds after questions and after responses) can be powerful prompts to individual thinking. Other strategies, such as paraphrasing and gentle prompting, assist people in going deeper in their thought and verbal responses.

4. *Creating a Culture of Inquiry* is about establishing and nurturing norms that promote powerful and productive conversations. Leaders attend to this element when they talk with members of their school communities about the value of inquiry, model inquiry, and build a climate of trust and mutual respect.

The second dimension of the LQQ Framework highlights four leadership functions that can be significantly enhanced through the intentional use of quality questioning.

1. *Maximizing* is related to leaders' efforts to develop individual and organizational capacity. Leaders who seek to maximize, focus on the ways and means to motivate and support individuals in reaching their potential.

2. *Mobilizing* is the process of getting people on board, of motivating them to act. Sometimes, the challenge is to mobilize individuals to accept a new mandate or program. Most often, it's to mobilize people to meet high expectations day-in-and-day-out in their work. Vision and purpose are the vehicles used by effective leaders to mobilize their constituents.

3. *Mediating* is the process whereby a leader helps individuals with differing perspectives understand one another's conflicting realities and forge a shared understanding of the situation so that they can work together. Mediating also involves helping individuals make personal meaning of a new idea or intervention so that they can decide whether or not (and how) to integrate these ideas into their own thinking.

4. *Monitoring* involves ongoing assessment of the extent to which individuals are aligning their actual performance to agreed-upon behaviors and are, as a consequence, on target to meet identified benchmarks or objectives.

These four featured functions are by no means inclusive of all leadership functions that can profit from focused questioning. They are, however, critically important in a school that values collaborative work patterns and is striving to become an authentic community of learners. Further, attention to these functions supports individuals' efforts to learn and grow as leaders.

Leaders Can Support Adult Learning Through Quality Questioning

Classroom teachers use quality questioning to focus and support student learning. In turn, today's education leaders increasingly use quality questioning to focus and support adult learning in schools. Ongoing learning is imperative in a culture characterized by continuous change, which requires each of us to examine and adapt our perspectives and practices if we are to sustain our effectiveness. *Learning* and *change* become synonymous within this cultural context, and leaders have an ever-increasing responsibility to design ongoing, job-embedded learning for all constituents. While this is a responsibility of all leaders, it is a particularly important one for education leaders, who are by definition leaders of learners. The most effective of these leaders intentionally seek opportunities to engage educators and education stakeholders in learning conversations that are driven by purposeful, well-focused questions. Quality questions are catalysts for productive reflection, dialogue, and learning throughout the school community.

2

Questioning as a Process

What Are the Essential Elements?

The art of asking open-ended questions that mediate meaning must be learned, practiced and refined. How leaders learn to frame questions either limits or enhances the group's ability to construct meaning and act in concert with others.

—Diane Zimmerman, "The Linguistics of Leadership"

FOCUS QUESTIONS

1. How do leaders craft quality questions?

2. What are the keys to presenting quality questions that engage all members of a learning community?

3. How does quality questioning deepen and extend the thinking of community members?

4. How do leaders encourage a culture of inquiry throughout the school and district?

Chapter 1 established the value of a school leader's using questioning to engage members of the school community, but all questions are not created equal. *Quality questions* are authentic; they might be posed to gain specific information, to understand another's point of view, to help others make personal meaning, to stimulate reflection and self-awareness, and to solve problems. Most of the issues in education have no simple answers; leaders who are open to learning will be asking questions throughout their entire careers.

As used in this book, *quality questioning* means much more than "asking questions." Quality questioning is a dynamic process that consists of multiple skills to achieve specific outcomes. The essential elements of the process involve the following:

- Framing or crafting a question
- Presenting the question effectively
- Extending thinking through a variety of verbal and nonverbal prompts
- Encouraging a schoolwide culture of inquiry in which "not knowing" is valued and questions are welcomed

How Do Leaders Craft Quality Questions?

There is, of course, no perfect question. Four guidelines, however, can help leaders frame quality questions: (1) identify the focus or topic of a question; (2) get clear about the purpose or desired outcome of the question (or question set); (3) decide on a process for engaging all appropriate parties, giving all an opportunity to voice their positions and to be heard respectfully; and (4) word the question so that it is simple and understandable.

Most quality questions require planning and intentionality. Yet, many questions must be formed spontaneously, as required by the situation. The more leaders practice creating questions using the four guidelines specified here, the easier it will be to pose quality questions, even without preparation time.

Identify Focus

Questions are powerful. They focus thinking. When asked a question, listeners begin thinking about the topic. Because the topic of the question most often determines what listeners think about, it is essential to be clear in your own mind about what it is you want to ask. Resist the temptation to string many topics together, even if they are related. Choose one focus for a question; pose it, and let the individual or group wrestle with it. If the question is well worded and open ended, chances are that others will introduce topics that are connected and related.

> Questions are quite powerful in focusing attention. When leaders ask questions, they send constituents on mental journeys—"quests"—in search of answers. The questions that a leader asks send messages about the focus of the organization, and they're indicators of what's of most concern to the leader.
>
> —Kouzes & Posner (2002, p. 91)

When we aren't sure of the topic we want to ask about, we tend to think as we talk. The result might be a rambling kind of question asking. For example, a well-intentioned leader who is seeking input from a group of teachers but has no clear focus might say something like, *"I'm concerned about student achievement. It seems that we have higher absenteeism than we did last year. And I'm hearing from some of you that students don't know how to use their time wisely. Do you think they would benefit from study skills?"* This question results from a lack of clarity about the focus for a question. What should the group think about—student achievement, absenteeism, or study skills?

The list of potential topics for fruitful discussion is endless. Based on what's happening in the school, a leader may want to initiate thought and discussion about a myriad of issues: the high rate of student absenteeism, meaningful involvement of parents and families, schoolwide agreement about the process for determining student grades, how to evaluate the use of formative assessment, alignment of the taught and tested curriculum, ways to improve math scores, and so forth. But sometimes, the apparent topic is only a symptom of something deeper. Let's take student absenteeism as an example. What is the real issue? Is it getting students to school? Keeping them in school? Making classes more engaging, relevant, and challenging so that students want to come to class? Is the issue related to teacher assumptions about the abilities of a given population in the school? Is the issue related to the values and culture of students in the school? Parent values? Probably the answer is yes—to all of these questions and more. A leader who has assembled a group of teachers to discuss student absenteeism already knows the focus of the group's inquiry—having a higher percentage of students in class, engaged in learning, and motivated to participate in learning. If the leader is to move the discussion beyond symptoms and address root causes and possible solutions, he or she can do so through quality questioning.

Clarify Purpose

Once a topic is identified, the leader's next task is to clarify intent: *What is my purpose in asking? What do I, as a leader, hope to accomplish?* The four leadership functions introduced in the Leading Through Quality Questioning (LQQ) Framework offer four potential purposes: *maximizing* or developing the potential of staff or members of the school community; *mobilizing* or motivating people to assume responsibility or to take action; promoting shared understanding or *mediating* conflict; and encouraging reflection, self-assessment, and *monitoring* of the work of the school. Conceptualizing questions by reference to these four purposes assists leaders in connecting emerging issues and topics to the broader challenge of leading for learning.

> *Questions that work have intention; they enable a group to get where it wants to go.*
>
> —Dorothy Strachan (2007, p. 8)

For example, an instructional coach who wants to mobilize staff to engage in more student-centered learning activities might ask a small group of teachers, "On a scale of one to five, how much do energy and engagement positively affect student learning?" The coach could also ask a companion question: "On a scale of one to five, how energized and engaged are your students in learning?" The coach might engage the group in discussing their responses by posing follow-up questions that promote sharing among the group, for example, "What is the evidence for your ratings?" "What kinds of activities appear to energize and engage your students?" "I'd like to hear about specific examples of times when your students were energized and engaged in learning—as well as times when the energy and engagement seemed particularly low."

If the coach wants to help teachers self-monitor, she might give positive feedback: "I noticed a high level of energy and enthusiasm during the cooperative learning activity on the division of fractions. Many students were talking—even arguing with one another, which is an indicator of true involvement—and I could see several of the groups thinking through the process." She might then ask for self-reflection in the form of a question: "Division of fractions is a difficult concept for many students to grasp; most simply memorize a formulaic strategy. I'm interested to know what you thought about the activity's success in promoting student understanding. In your opinion, how did it go?" Follow up with a question that leads teachers to extend their thinking: "How will you assess students' understanding?"

Use Open-Ended Versus Closed Questions

Chapters 3 through 6 include examples of questions that leaders can pose as they exercise each of the four leadership functions described in the LQQ Framework in Chapter 1 (Figure 1.1). Note that questions designed to maximize, motivate, mediate, and monitor are rarely closed questions. A closed question usually calls for a short answer, a piece of information, an opinion, or a simple yes or no. An open-ended question, on the other hand, promotes thinking and encourages multiple possible responses. The goal in asking open-ended questions is to promote individual buy in, discovery, and ownership of potential solutions.

The examples of closed and open-ended questions in Resource A illustrate why and how the way questions are asked can influence the nature of a discussion. As you examine this material, pay particular attention to the length and thoughtfulness of the teacher's responses. The teacher whose thinking is activated by open-ended questions is more likely to follow through on the leader's ideas because open questions help people overcome resistance to movement and change.

Posing open-ended questions can be challenging. Because most of the questions posed in classrooms are closed questions that call for a right answer, many of us educators are most familiar with these kinds of questions. Closed questions are a mechanism for control. When we pose more thought-provoking questions, we don't know where student (or faculty) thinking might go. In addition, open-ended questions require more time—both in the preparation of the questions and in the posing and answering of them. Look at the difference in the length of the two conversations in Resource A. Closed questions clearly use less time. In this book, we make the case that closed questions are not as effective and that the time devoted to asking quality questions is well spent.

Select a Process

Quality questioning extends beyond the question itself. To frame a quality question, leaders must identify the context in which they plan to pose the question and then select an appropriate process to elicit responses. Most questioning occurs within the context of routine conversations: *A principal encounters a teacher in the hallway and asks for an update on a current project. An instructional coach interacts with classroom teachers during their planning block about a literacy strategy presented in a recent professional development session. An assistant principal meets with the parent of a student who is chronically tardy.* The daily situations in which we employ questioning are countless.

Almost all of the practices highlighted in this book apply to the emerging, authentic conversations we engage in every day. Each of us can improve our use of best practice in these situations. Additionally, we argue that leaders can capitalize on the power of quality questions by planning for their use in scheduled meetings and community gatherings; that is, in more formal settings. In these cases, leaders can be intentional in choosing a structured group process that affords opportunities for all individual voices to be heard, encourages all individuals to formulate responses, and promotes the sharing and honoring of diverse views.

Using new processes to lead conversations will require leaders to break question-asking habits that are well established in school culture. In most classrooms, for example, the typical pattern is (1) the teacher asks a question and (2) calls on one student to answer, guaranteeing that few students are engaged in thinking about the question and formulating a response. In most classrooms, more than a fourth of the students never speak (Jones, 1990; Sadker & Sadker, 1985). The results of this practice are inequity in response opportunities, differential teacher expectations for learning, and resultant gaps in student achievement.

This same pattern occurs in many adult meetings, such as grade-level, departmental, faculty, and PTA meetings. A few people articulate their thoughts in response to the questions posed. Others in the group tune out, either silently agreeing with their more verbal colleagues or—more frequently—internally processing different views that never get expressed or that are voiced after the meeting. Such passive participation in the group creates undercurrents that can generate resistance, negativity, and conflict. Fortunately, with planning, leaders can help groups to avoid these negative consequences. Leaders can select strategies that engage all members of a group and help them offer opinions in a manner that ensures that their voices are heard and valued.

> *Some of us never have been invited to share our ideas and opinions. From early school days and now as adults, we've been instructed to be quiet so others can tell us what to think. . . . The experiences have left us feeling hesitant to speak, and frightened of each other.*
>
> —Margaret Wheatley (2002, p. 24)

In our earlier book, *Quality Questioning: Research-Based Practice to Engage Every Learner* (2005), we suggest that using alternate response formats in classroom settings can actively engage all students in thinking and responding to questions. Examples of alternate response formats include Think-Pair-Share, Signals, Peoplegraph, Interview Design, Synectics, and Fishbowl. When teachers use such processes, all students are accountable to formulate a response. Sometimes, they speak only to a partner; at other times, in small groups. Sometimes, their responses are anonymous; at other times, they respond verbally to a group or partner.

Many of the same processes are appropriate for meetings of adults (or meetings of adults and students) as they consider schoolwide issues. See Resource B for descriptions of various processes you can use to engage all participants in thinking and expressing their ideas.

How does the selection of a particular process impact the formation of the question? Let's say, for example, that you have decided to use Interview Design, a protocol that you will read more about in Chapters 6 and 7. You will need to create four or five quality questions that stimulate thinking and reflection on the topic at hand. These questions must be appropriate for individuals to answer via interview. If you decide to use

Data on Display (featured in Chapter 3), the questions need to help participants identify and think about the discrepancy between what they believe and how they act. To prepare a question for Think-Pair-Share, you should prepare a prompt to stimulate thinking that is not limited to a single right answer. And for Peoplegraph, you will need a statement with which it is possible to agree or disagree, one that prompts individuals to demonstrate diverse points of view on a single topic.

Word Carefully

One important reason to spend time formulating questions before asking them is to ensure that they communicate what is intended. Table 2.1 lists a number of common errors to avoid in crafting questions. Remember: Words communicate content, but they also communicate information about the relationship between the speaker and the listener. The examples given in the table demonstrate how some questions can unintentionally diminish the value of the potential respondent, increase defensiveness, and cut off discussion and open sharing.

As you put final touches on a question, read it aloud, especially if it is to be posed orally. This can help you determine whether the question will be readily understandable to listeners.

Table 2.1 Common Errors in Questioning

Common Errors to Avoid	Description	Example
Jargon and difficult or inappropriate words	Use of educational jargon can cause a question to be unclear to all, but especially to noneducators (i.e., community members, parents, or students).	*Our school improvement leadership team has been studying the results of the criterion-referenced state assessments, and we have detected a recurrent trend in certain demographic groups outperforming others. How could we best address this situation?*
Stacked questions, also called serialized or "machine gun" questions	Rather than posing a single question, we sometimes ask question after question, trying to clarify our own thinking. People don't know which question to think about when there is no clear focus.	*We've got a lot of complaints about homework coming from parents. Are you all giving appropriate amounts? Do parents have access to the assignments on the Web site? Do you work together, so you know when major assignments are due from other teachers? What can we do about this problem? Have you got any suggestions?*

(Continued)

Table 2.1   (Continued)

Common Errors to Avoid	Description	Example
Double-barreled questions	This type of question requires respondents to answer two questions; but it's worded as if there is only one question at issue, making it difficult to answer.	*Do you think we should have two opportunities for parent-teacher conferences this fall or just one that involves students and has some icebreaker activities?* *(What if the respondent wants two—and also desires student involvement?)*
Leading questions	Such questions are worded to suggest that only one response is appropriate. They do not promote thinking or suggest a safe environment for responding.	*Don't you think it would be better to assign grades based on test scores and participation rates?*
Using one's position of authority to create inequity	The question is worded to communicate that the asker is in a position of authority and has the "right" answer; respondents are expected to agree.	*I think we should have parent conferences during evening hours; so does the superintendent. What do you think?*
Using loaded words	This error is related to the previous two—leading questions and using authority. Loaded questions use words that are "loaded" with innuendo and signal that there is a "correct" answer or response.	*Don't you think it would be smart to give students a warm-up or sponge activity when they arrive?*
Focusing on the negative	A question can move people to positive thinking—or to more negative thinking.	*Why do we have so many students scoring in the lowest quartile?*

What Are the Keys to Presenting Questions to Engage All Members of a Learning Community?

A leader can formulate a quality question, but it will not be effective unless it is asked so that people hear it, feel comfortable answering it, and believe that what they have to say will be valued. This section focuses on an often-ignored aspect of quality questioning: effective presentation of questions.

Plan for Equitable Engagement of Participants

Leaders should strive to nurture the active and equitable engagement of all community members in both formal and informal conversations. Achieving this goal requires strategic and intentional work that helps people understand the purpose and rationale for equitable involvement. Following are some suggestions to help accomplish full and equitable engagement:

- Talk to faculty, parent groups, and student groups about the phenomenon of some people talking more than others in groups. Let them know this is normal, but that you are interested in hearing from everyone. Engage in a discussion about the challenge this poses. Have group members consider what each can do to assist in ensuring that all have an opportunity to participate.
- Plan for where to position yourself in relationship to the group. Just as a good teacher might do, move around the room so that you can see different people and different parts of the room. In a small-group meeting, make eye contact with everyone. Think about how to keep track of who has spoken and how frequently.
- Use icebreakers and other "moving around" activities so that the same people are not sitting together at every meeting. This will not only expand their viewpoints but will also discourage sidebar conversations.
- Think about room arrangement before a meeting. If working with a large group, provide small tables so that participants can talk to one another in groups of four or five before entering a large-group discussion. If tables are not available, move desks together so that participants are in learning groups.
- Limit the length of presentation. Surprisingly, at many faculty meetings only a very few people speak—and those are usually the formal leaders. The 20/80 rule suggests that leaders should not plan to speak any more than 20 percent of the time; other participants should be engaged in talking 80 percent of the time.

- Pose the question as part of a process in which everyone will be given the opportunity to respond. Use the strategies described throughout the book (and in Resource B) to engage multiple participants in thinking and talking.

Set the Context

Beth's husband is hard-of-hearing. Sometimes, when she asks a question, he doesn't understand. But it's not always because he hasn't heard the question. Sometimes it's because he hasn't heard what was said *before* the question was asked; that is, he doesn't have a *context* to help him make sense of the question.

For all of us, it's true that if we don't have background information and aren't prepared to "hear" the question, it can be hard to make sense of it. We have found, as facilitators, that it is almost always helpful to give a sentence or two of context setting before posing a question. This not only helps participants understand what the question is about but also gives them time to tune in to the question so that they are paying attention by the time it is asked. Context setting also helps to even the playing field by giving everyone the same background information.

Instead of asking, *Should we have students engaged in parent conferences?* a leader might introduce the question by giving some background and common vocabulary: *Ellie and James have been learning a lot about something called student-led conferences. They have shared with us the results that other schools have gotten when they implemented these: higher rates of parent attendance, greater understanding of grades by students, increased sense of student responsibility for the learning process. But, they have also shared with us the increased amount of teacher time required to help students be fully prepared. Right now, I'd like to hear where you are in thinking about having students engaged in parent conferences.*

Ask With Interest in the Question: Pause, as You Ask, for Emphasis

We all know the difference between a monotone delivery of a question (making it seem that the question is not interesting even to the person asking it) and a question that is delivered in such a way as to convey its importance. Quality questioners ask with interest in others' thoughts and ideas; they emphasize or accent key words. Pausing during the asking of a question gives a leader time to scan participants' faces and assess their levels of engagement: Are they with me? Do they seem to understand? Are there distractions happening that I should take into account?

Look again at the question you read two paragraphs ago about student-led conferences. The introductory remarks are long. If this information comes out quickly, with no pauses, it's likely that people will have difficulty following the train of thought. In fact, for a question this detailed, it might be important to present some of the content visually—for example, bulleted on flip-chart paper or displayed on a PowerPoint slide. Even with the addition of visual aids, you can help listeners by pausing occasionally as you speak. Such pauses give emphasis to important details—and they demonstrate that you believe the ideas under discussion are worth thinking about.

Ask and Then Pause; Wait in Silence

In our society, silence is not golden. We rush and hurry as a matter of course; many of us have come to believe that silence is a waste of time. There is compelling research, however, that demonstrates the importance of short periods of silence. In research done in K–12 classrooms, Mary Budd Rowe (1986) discovered that if teachers wait three to five seconds after asking a question before calling on a student to answer, students answer more confidently and more completely. She called this pause Wait Time 1. Rowe also discovered that with the addition of Wait Time 2 (a pause after a student responds and before a teacher comments on the response), the benefits to learning increase even more. She found more students participating (including low-achieving students, who typically do not answer questions), giving longer answers, and asking more questions. For a more complete review of the research, see Walsh and Sattes (2005, pp. 80–86).

In our own experiences of facilitating adult learning and problem solving, we have found similar results with the use of Wait Times 1 and 2. We have learned the hard way that one can't just "do" wait time; participants will be uncomfortable with the silence unless they understand the reasons for it. Initially, in some of our trainings, when we used Wait Time 2 (waiting for 3 seconds after someone responded before commenting), we got some very strange looks from participants. Once, during a pause, someone asked us directly, "What's the matter? Is my answer wrong?" The question made us realize that adults—like students—need to understand that we don't intend to comment immediately, that we are creating space for the respondent and other participants to think about what has been said. Ideally, the discussion leader won't be the one to comment; rather, participants will be stimulated to add ideas or ask questions. We can certainly attest to the power of intentional silence to stimulate thought and to more fully engage participants.

Ask With Interest in the Answer; Use Listening Skills That Demonstrate Sincere Interest

J. T. Dillon (1988), a long-time student of classroom questioning, advises educators to "ask with interest in the student's answer." He contends that most teachers (and we've been as guilty as the next) most frequently ask with interest in *their own* answer—not the student's answer. We believe this is doubly important for leaders: We must listen with interest to the respondent's thinking.

How do we demonstrate this interest? Much of it is nonverbal. In listening to another's answer, maintain eye contact. Lean toward the respondent, sometimes gesturing for them to say more. Nod and look interested, hanging on every word. Verbal responses also demonstrate listening. After a participant responds to a question, wait three to five seconds to be sure the person is finished, then elaborate on the comment, rephrasing it and extending it. There is no higher praise—or demonstration that a person was heard clearly—than when the group leader talks in a positive way about what was said. In addition, hearken back to what a participant said earlier ("Do you remember when Mark gave us an example of scaffolding students' answers?") before adding a comment about it. Bringing up Mark's earlier response demonstrates not only that he was heard but also that his response was valued enough to refer to later. This is a powerful way to demonstrate listening. It is a difficult skill to develop; however, the dividends are well worth the effort.

Ask With Authenticity, Curiosity, Openness, and Respect

Our core values affect whether and how we pose questions, engage participants equitably, invite responses, and respond to them appropriately. The mind-set with which we ask will determine the result—both for us and for the person to whom we pose a question. In *Leading with Questions*, Michael Marquardt (2005) cites Marilee Adams (2004), who postulates two different mind-sets from which we can ask questions: judger and learner. Those with a learner mind-set are interested in possibilities and hope; they are flexible; they listen objectively; they search for unusual and creative answers. The judger mind-set, on the other hand, tends to ask with his or her own answer in mind; can be reactive, blaming, defensive, and even attacking. Judging attitudes tend to cause people to be defensive, wary, and less than open.

Quality questioning requires four habits of mind that are related to the learner mind-set: authenticity, curiosity, openness, and respect. Table 2.2 describes these habits of mind and how they contribute to the quality-questioning process.

Table 2.2   Habits of Mind That Promote Quality Questioning

Habit of Mind	Contribution to Quality Questioning
A leader who values questioning as an important way to engage others and stimulate thinking exhibits the following ways of being:	*When a leader exhibits this habit of mind, members of a school community are more willing and likely to*
Authentic: The leader is genuine, real, and clear about intentions; has no hidden agendas, is fully present; exhibits consistency between words and deeds; is believable; sets an example of questioning and listening to learn; and asks questions from a position of wondering and not knowing.	Trust the leader and, by extension, other members of the community; give authentic and honest responses when afforded the opportunity; admit vulnerabilities, knowing there will not be repercussions; and be willing to try questioning and listening as a way of learning and leading.
Curious: The leader wonders, asks true questions, listens to learn, believes in exploring ideas, sees the school as a place that can always be better, believes that everyone has something to teach, does not prejudge answers, probes to fully understand what is behind a comment, and collects data and uses them to make decisions and to make meaning.	Enjoy asking questions, hearing different points of view, and collecting data to search for answers; believe that questions help guide improvement; know that learning is a process and no one ever "arrives"; become increasingly honest in answering; and be willing to take risks of not knowing.
Open: The leader is interested in what others think (and why) rather than in hearing a specific "right" answer, is able to withhold judgment and keep an open mind, shares self with others and is willing to admit not knowing, trusts the process and relinquishes control, and is willing to expose his or her own uncertainties and vulnerabilities.	Be more open to diverse points of view; be willing to explore possibilities, rather than "win" arguments; and answer honestly, knowing that others are accepting of their ideas.
Respectful: The leader believes in ensuring equity of voice, acts in a fair and unbiased way, believes every viewpoint has merit, demonstrates respect by listening and by waiting between comments, clarifies group norms and consciously clarifies issues that require confidentiality, encourages direct interaction between participants, and does not repeat answers but asks participants to speak in a loud and clear voice.	Meet with other community members as peers, not in roles of superior and inferior, believe everyone has a voice and a contribution, see that all are heard and respected, take more ownership, develop better listening skills and use wait time before speaking, help to establish and monitor important norms of conversation, share responsibility and ownership of new learnings, commit to other members of the community, and support others.

How Does Quality Questioning Deepen and Extend Thinking?

Whether leaders are asking questions to individuals or to groups, the question and initial response are just the beginning of the thinking process. Most often, we can listen to what's said—and listen to what's *not* said—and give a verbal or nonverbal prompt to encourage individuals to continue and deepen their thinking.

Use Nonverbal Prompts

Listening is primarily communicated nonverbally. The listening skills suggested earlier in this chapter apply equally to extending thinking. Remember Wait Time 2, in which the three- to-five-second silence after an answer is given? Try it. Use nonverbal cues to communicate your interest in what a person says, but resist the initial temptation to interrupt, add your own opinion, or ask anything else immediately. Instead, say nothing. Wait to see if, without any verbal prompts, more is forthcoming.

Wait Time 2 is almost always helpful, but sometimes it seems like a miracle in a difficult situation. A colleague of ours, Earl Wiman, shared the story of using Wait Time 2 with an irate parent. The parent stormed into Principal Wiman's office ready to "take his head off," in Earl's words. As the parent talked, Earl listened. He looked at the parent encouragingly, saying nothing, conveying interest and attention, but waiting in silence. The parent paused occasionally, Earl continued to listen quietly, and the parent continued talking. When the parent had finished, he stood, shook Earl's hand, and said, "I just want to thank you for all your help in this matter." The parent, essentially, had solved his own problem. And Earl had a friend forever!

One of the easiest human acts is also the most healing. Listening to someone. Simply listening. Not advising or coaching, but silently and fully listening.

—Margaret Wheatley (2007, p. 88)

Sometimes the silence allows room for a group to take responsibility. We were once facilitating group dialogue when—it seemed out of the blue—one of the participants said, with a lot of emotion, "I was awake almost all night. I can't shake the feeling that we're doing this thinking and talking for nothing. I'm afraid nothing will come of it; this will be just one more effort that doesn't make a difference." As facilitators of the process, we could have viewed the comment as an attack on our process; but, being familiar with wait time and trusting in the group, both of us waited. (Also, to be honest, we were so stunned that we were speechless!) In our silence, we clearly were considering the comment; neither of us moved to be dismissive of what was an important comment to this participant. After what seemed an eternity—but likely was less than one minute—one of the group members spoke. "I know we've tried many things, and they never seem to last. But I think if we make the commitment, we can sustain this." Other members of the group spoke then; it was a deeply moving experience. How glad we were that we had not jumped in to diffuse the situation; the decision to continue with the process was really the group's decision, not ours. Many are the times we've reflected on that experience to affirm the value of wait time. Without the silence, we believe we would have spoken prematurely. How much better for colleagues to talk directly to one another!

Use Follow-Up Questions (Verbal Prompts)

Silence is not the only option for encouraging thinking. Sometimes, the response to our question causes us to want to comment or ask another question. There are several reasons for this follow-up:

- *To expose and get behind thinking.* Ask a question to more fully understand respondents' perspectives, where they are coming from, and what assumptions are implicit in their thinking.
- *To confirm understanding of a speaker's statement.* To fully understand what another person has said, summarize, restate, or paraphrase his or her response.
- *To clarify a response; to elicit extension or expansion of thinking.* When someone makes a statement but doesn't fully explain it, encourage the person to take that thinking deeper; ask a question that will extend the individual's thinking.
- *To encourage reflection and self-assessment.* Ask one or more members of a group to assess where they are in their thinking about the topic under discussion.

In asking a question or making a comment, and doing so without judgment, leaders not only solicit additional information; they also show interest in what has been said. There are many instances in which it is more helpful to probe than to assume you understand or to make a statement that judges the comment. Examples of possible probes and prompts appear in Table 2.3.

> *Ask for an example or an anecdote to clarify a response whenever someone gives you a general answer to a question. Examples and anecdotes make a session more vibrant and immediate; they are the spice in the conversation, the hook that enables others to identify with a particular situation or experience.*
>
> —Dorothy Strachan (2007, p. 61)

Table 2.3 Follow-Up Questions and Comments to Extend Thinking

Purpose of Question or Comment	Examples and Stems
To expose and get behind thinking	1. Help me understand what you were thinking when you said . . . 2. How did you figure that out? 3. Can you help me understand how you reached that conclusion? 4. How did you know? 5. What assumptions are you making when you say that? 6. What experiences have you had that lead you to this conclusion? 7. What data did you use to reach that inference? 8. What do you mean by . . . ? 9. What criteria did you use to make that assessment? 10. How does your perspective compare to . . . ? 11. Have we included all the perspectives that we need to include? 12. Is there anyone who has a different perspective who has not yet spoken?
To confirm our own understanding of the speaker's statement	1. Let's see if I've got this right. (*Then summarize your understanding of what the speaker said.*) 2. I understood you to say . . . Am I interpreting your comments correctly? 3. So you think that . . . ?
To elicit extension or expansion of thinking	1. How else might we think about . . . ? 2. What if . . .? 3. Can you give an example? 4. Can you be more specific? 5. How could we go about finding out? 6. How are you planning to go about . . . ? 7. I follow your logic. What's best to do at this point? 8. I'd like to hear more of your thinking. 9. Please say more. 10. What can we infer from . . . ? 11. What do you mean by the word . . . ? 12. Keep going. I'd like to hear more. 13. Let's take this a little further. Can you say more?

Purpose of Question or Comment	Examples and Stems
To encourage self-assessment	1. Which part are you sure of? What is still puzzling you?
	2. What did you learn when . . . ?
	3. Is that an observation or a hypothesis?
	4. How do you feel about . . . ?
	5. What can we learn from this?
	6. Do we have all the facts?
	7. Is there other evidence we might try to collect?
	8. How does this work for you?
	9. Where are you in relation to this topic?

Notice that none of these prompts begins with *why* even though many of them are seeking the answer to why. *Why* questions tend to put people on the defensive; they discourage openness. If the content is emotional, this is even more likely to be true. Turn the *why* into a *what* question; you can ask the same thing but get a better response. For example, instead of asking, *Why did you (do that)?* say, *Tell me what you were thinking that led up to (doing that).* Instead of asking, *Why don't you want to do that?* ask, *What comes to mind when you consider doing that?*

How Do Leaders Encourage a Culture of Inquiry Throughout the School or District, Inviting Questions From Members of Their Learning Communities?

Quality questioning can play a powerful role in transforming the fabric of school life for educators and students alike. Such a transformation begins with a focus on student learning and thinking. By focusing everyone on this central matter and nurturing a culture of inquiry, education leaders can develop individual and collective capacity to monitor and adjust responses to critical issues within the school community.

Focus on Student Learning and Thinking

In *Developing More Curious Minds,* John Barell (2003) quotes Carl Sagan: "Both skepticism and wonder are skills that need honing and practice.

Their harmonious marriage within the mind of every school child ought to be a principal goal of public education" (p. 17). Barell contends that for a variety of reasons—including fear, defensiveness, preserving the status quo, and being polite—we spend little time helping our students learn to be curious, to ask questions. Research on classroom questioning practices confirms Barell's notion that little time is spent on student questions. Teachers ask most of the questions in school; students ask fewer than five percent of the questions. His book, which is about stimulating curiosity and inquisitiveness among students, presents a challenge to thoughtful educators about the need for change in traditional teaching practices.

> All our knowledge results from questions, which is another way of saying that question-asking is our most important intellectual tool.
>
> —Neil Postman (1979, p. 140)

Quality questions are an important life skill: They stimulate thinking and learning; they can engage students in powerful learning. In a previous book, *Quality Questioning: Research-Based Practice to Engage Every Learner* (2005), we focus on the skills and beliefs that are needed to foster questioning in the classroom.

In this book, our focus turns to the leader's skills. One of the most compelling reasons for the leader's use of questioning to foster and stimulate thinking is to *model inquiry* as a personal and professional value. In schools where leaders operate by command-and-control procedures, as is typical in traditional organizations, teachers will also tend to operate that way, developing complacent and passive students. On the other hand, in a school where a leader uses questions—to foster collaboration in generating new ideas and solutions, to model continuous learning, to seek to understand others' perceptions and beliefs, to gather data to measure effectiveness—it is much more likely that a culture of inquiry will be embedded in the school and present in classrooms and staff meetings alike.

Encourage a Culture of Inquiry

The benefits of a leader creating a culture of inquiry, as outlined in Chapter 1, include collaboration, willingness to share, openness to learn, acceptance of shared responsibility, a sense of accountability, and a focus on learning—both for students and for adults. Following are five strategies school leaders can use to change the culture of a school to one that encourages questioning.

1. Model quality questioning.
2. Encourage questioning at every opportunity; build questioning into every meeting and conversation.

3. Reward and acknowledge quality questioning.

4. Make the values of inquiry explicit.

5. Provide training for quality questioning.

> *Probably the most important—and the most difficult—job of the school-based reformer is to change the prevailing culture of a school. The school's culture dictates, in no uncertain terms, 'the way we do things around here.' Ultimately, a school's culture has far more influence on life and learning in the schoolhouse than the state department of education, the superintendent, the school board, or even the principal can ever have.*
>
> —Roland Barth (2001, p. 7)

1. Model Quality Questioning

In *The Leadership Challenge*, Kouzes and Posner (2002) suggest five practices for exemplary leadership. The first is "model the way," which, among other things, means that leaders' actions are in alignment with their values. If a leader values inquiry and continuous learning, that leader will model seeking, questioning, listening, and learning.

> *Leading through asking of questions is a culture change that is not easy to bring about—we often prefer to talk with exclamation marks than with interrogatory ones!*
>
> —Michael Marquardt (2005, p. 109)

When leaders ask with authenticity and listen with true interest, they demonstrate respect for others' thinking, ideas, and opinions. Kouzes and Posner (2002) suggest that leaders conduct a self-audit on this topic. As part of the audit, leaders might ask for feedback on specific questioning and listening behaviors. For instance, they might ask someone to keep a tally during a meeting of parents or teachers:

- How many questions did I ask? (Aim for quality over quantity.)
- Who spoke during the meeting? (Your goal is to engage all participants.)
- How much did I speak? (Remember the suggestion of 20% or less?)
- How much did I listen quietly and attentively? (This goal might be 80%.)

When leaders begin to develop or heighten a culture of inquiry in schools, they will likely encounter resistance. People are used to hearing answers, not questions. Teachers and other staff may not believe the leader is really open to hearing new ideas; they may think the questioning is a test of whether or not they are in line with the leadership stance. Marquardt (2005) suggests that strong resistance comes from an existing culture that has bred "answer-dependency" and "telling-dependency" (p. 109). Answer dependency comes from the experience of being rewarded for an attitude of "tell me what to do; I'll do it." Telling dependency is related. It is especially strong in schools, coming from the ingrained belief that when someone asks you a question, you should respond with an answer. We rarely think of turning the question back to the person who brought the question.

> *When someone comes in to see me with a problem or question, I always try to turn it around and ask them what they think about the problem.*
>
> —Michael Marquardt (2005, p. 107)

2. Encourage Questioning at Every Opportunity

Create opportunities for people to pose questions. For example, you might open a learning session with this charge: What did you face this week that challenged you? Write down three things that you'd like to learn more about, related to teaching and learning. Use simple structures such as Thinking Routines, which are presented on the Visible Thinking section of Harvard's Project Zero Web site (Palmer, Perkins, Ritchhart, & Tishman, n.d.). There, you will find strategies you can use "to make thinking visible within the context of learning." For example, a strategy called "Connect Extend Challenge" prompts participants' reflection at the close of a learning session by posing the following three questions:

- How are the ideas and information presented and reviewed today CONNECTED to what you already knew and believed?
- What new ideas did you get that EXTENDED or pushed your thinking in new directions?
- What is still CHALLENGING or confusing for you to get your mind around? What questions, wonderings, or puzzles do you now have? (Palmer, Perkins, Ritchhart, & Tishman, n.d.)

The establishment of a professional learning community, the purpose of which is to learn with and from one another within a school, often gets stalled because faculty end up talking about facilitators' questions—not their own. Our experience is that a group of teachers often has difficulty formulating questions. This is amazing when you consider the complexity of the job of teaching! Questions such as, *What can I do to help an eighth grader learn to read?* are rarely heard in the faculty lounge. Rather, you might hear, *What do they expect! I've got an eighth grader who can't read!*

> *We should be proud to say, "I don't know!" Too often we are embarrassed by our ignorance. Unfortunately, schools do not always nurture that sense of being in a state of doubt and then searching for answers.*
>
> —John Barell (2003, p. 15)

The questioning culture, once accepted, can help to create trust and positive relationships. But developing such a culture takes time. Be patient. Adults need to learn new ways of thinking and acting in order to feel comfortable with this new style of communication. Only with a sense of safety will a teacher be able to pose a question that is troubling her: *I don't know how to work with English language learners. I feel like I'm not reaching them. Has anyone else had this experience? Can anyone offer suggestions?*

If the idea of leading through questioning is new to a school or district, begin by asking questions one on one in order to develop trust. When posing a question to a larger group, allow people to talk with colleagues before ideas are shared with the whole group. Strategies like Think-Pair-Share or Say Something (see Resource B) provide people with the experience of talking openly and honestly and exploring what they think with one other person.

3. Reward and Acknowledge Quality Questioning

As leaders encourage a culture of inquiry, a sphere where not knowing has value, they will encounter questions that are not quality questions. For example, *With all the baggage these kids bring to school, what do you expect from them?* These kinds of questions are posed defensively; the person asking is not open to thinking about the issue in a different way. The asker thinks he or she already knows the answer; it's one of a variety that leaders hear every day: Students can't learn if they don't try; students can't learn if their families don't value education; students can't learn if . . . The excuses—and the unquestioned underlying assumptions—can seem never ending.

The leader who is interested in maximizing and mobilizing a faculty to address these kinds of difficult issues needs to be willing to tackle the "nondiscussables." Using strategies such as data on display and five whys, leaders can begin to help faculty members develop a sense of wonder that might be expressed as *What if . . . ?* or *What more can we do?* When these questions are posed, leaders need to be ready to accept them as genuine.

Informally thank those who are willing to express questions that lead us to possibilities instead of dead ends. Eventually, when the culture is changing and people are aware of the vision for continuous learning through inquiry, make the recognition formal.

4. Make the Values of Inquiry Explicit

Changing a school culture is difficult work. Leaders nurture positive changes when they share their vision and are open with their staff and faculty. Talk about what you are trying and why. Don't tell people to ask questions, rather, ask them about it: *What might happen, during our department meetings, if we were more intentional about asking questions instead of conducting business as usual?*

In classrooms, we recommend that teachers establish norms for this new kind of thinking and being in school and that they teach these norms explicitly to their students, through discussion and clarification of what each norm means. We believe it is equally important to introduce adults to a set of norms that represent "the way we intend to do business" in the school or district. Sample norms appear in the chart below.

NORMS THAT SUPPORT A CULTURE OF INQUIRY

1. All of us know more than any one of us.

2. Invite and value questions.

3. "Think times" contribute to depth and clarity in thinking.

4. Honest feedback supports continuous learning and growth.

5. Listening to understand another's point of view is essential for productive communication.

6. Questioning and thinking nurture shared commitment and responsible action.

Each of these norms could be introduced to a faculty, allowing some time for discussion of what each might look like if adhered to, the value of each, and the amount of change that will be required to accomplish each. When faculty are in on it, and when they understand the value and rationale of a culture of questioning, they are likely to try harder to help create it. When teachers experience the value of such a culture, hopefully they will work to establish a similar one in their classrooms.

5. Provide Training for Quality Questioning

Quality questioning is simple, but it's not easy. Becoming an authentic questioner—one who listens well, probes to understand another's point of view, and looks for questions that could help him or her become an improved teacher—requires a lifelong commitment. Consider providing training for teachers, staff, students, and parents so that the school community becomes skilled in posing questions as well as listening to and valuing other points of view.

Quality questioning doesn't come naturally or easily for those of us who have learned to "go along to get along." Roland Barth (2001) suggests that the culture in most schools is one of caution (p. 185). He writes that all too often, those of us in schools don't want to take risks, don't want to assume responsibility, and don't want to try something new. Leaders can act to change this dynamic by giving members of the school community opportunities to learn together, with reflective feedback after a meeting. Such experiences can strengthen the resolve of a group to adopt quality questioning as a way of working together.

3

Maximizing

How Can Leaders Increase Individual and Collective Capacity?

The signs of outstanding leadership appear primarily among the followers. Are the followers reaching their potential? Are they learning? Serving? Do they achieve the required results? Do they change with grace? Manage conflict?

—Max De Pree, *Leadership Is an Art*

FOCUS QUESTIONS

1. What does maximizing mean in the context of school leadership? What are some important facets of maximizing?

2. What is the relationship between quality questioning and the development of individual and organizational capacity?

3. What kinds of questions facilitate the development of individual and organizational potential?

Hank, who is beginning his second year as principal of Magnolia Middle School, is concerned, but not surprised, by the results of the previous year's state assessment. Hank's analysis reveals a significant gap between the achievement of students qualifying for free and reduced-price meals and that of other students in the school, which serves 763 students. As he examines individual student data, Hank replays the reasons offered by faculty and staff when he discussed the report card grades of these same students. "You know, these kids just don't get the support they need at home." "These kids don't have a strong work ethic. I can't make them learn." "What do you expect? She hasn't been on grade level since the second grade."

Hank believes that the 45 individuals who teach and work at Magnolia are hard-working, well-intentioned individuals. He suspects that the excuse making has long been a part of the school's culture and that this norm undermines the belief to which most faculty give lip service; namely, that all students can learn. Further, he believes this excuse-making mentality affects individual and collective beliefs regarding efficacy. He fears that many faculty members do not believe that their individual and collective efforts can make a difference for these kids. He asks himself, What if every member of this faculty truly believed that they had the capacity to change the course of underperforming students' academic achievement? What results would we see on next year's state assessment? Why don't our faculty members have a stronger sense of self-efficacy? What would it take for them to examine their beliefs in an honest and critical fashion? Do all of our teachers have the pedagogical knowledge and skills needed to connect with all students?

Hank is committed to maximizing the effectiveness of each individual within the Magnolia school community—adults and students alike. He believes that one of his responsibilities as a leader is to help individuals reach their personal potential, particularly as it contributes to organizational effectiveness. He agrees with Max DePree (1989), who writes that organizational "effectiveness comes about through enabling others to reach their potential—both their personal potential and their organizational potential" (pp. 19–20). Hank understands that learning and growth are keys to this process— and that adult learning, like student learning, occurs in both the cognitive and the affective domains.

In fact, Hank speculates that attitudes and beliefs as well as pedagogical knowledge are contributors to the challenge represented in the school's test results. Figure 3.1 displays Hank's mental model for thinking about the challenges of maximizing the performance of his faculty.

| Figure 3.1 | The Maximizing Leader's Mental Model |

	Individual Teacher	**Collective**
	Dimension 1	*Dimension 2*
Values and Attitudes	**Self-efficacy:** "To what extent does each teacher believe that his or her effort makes a difference in the performance of students?" **Continuous learning and improvement:** "In what ways do individuals exhibit a belief that they can improve their performance every day?"	**Collective efficacy:** "What evidence suggests a belief on the part of our faculty that what they do (or fail to do) makes a difference in the performance of our students?" **Collective responsibility:** "Is there a schoolwide belief that each staff member is responsible for the learning and behavior of every student in our school?" **Collaborative culture:** "Do we behave as if all of us know more than any one of us?" **Mutual trust and respect:** "Are we, as a learning community, open to giving and receiving assistance from one another?"
	Dimension 3	*Dimension 4*
Knowledge and Skills	**Depth of content knowledge:** "To what extent do individual teachers have a deep understanding of the content for each of the courses or classes they teach?" **Student engagement:** "How effectively does each teacher engage each student in thinking and learning?" **Nurturing a positive learning culture:** "To what extent do teachers guide students in assuming responsibility for their own behavior and respect for self and others?"	**Group dialogue and communication skills:** "How skilled are members of our learning community in listening, questioning, respecting differences, suspending judgment, and voicing?" **Consensus-building skills:** "To what extent do faculty members know how to build a shared understanding of important issues?"

Hank's thinking, as illustrated in Figure 3.1, suggests that a leader who seeks to build individual and organizational capacity thinks multidimensionally. A maximizing leader considers factors related to the individual as well as factors related to the broader community or the collective. He or she also recognizes that knowledge and skills, in addition to beliefs and attitudes, contribute to effectiveness.

Robert Marzano and colleagues (Marzano, Waters, & McNulty, 2005) identify *optimizer* as one of the 21 responsibilities of school leaders associated with increased student achievement. These authors' view of the optimizer function is closely related to our leadership function of maximizing. They define it as the "extent to which the leader inspires others and is the driving force when implementing challenging innovation" (p. 56). Their meta-analysis of research identified the following specific behaviors associated with this leadership function:

- Inspiring teachers to accomplish things that may be beyond their grasp
- Being the driving force behind major initiatives
- Portraying a positive attitude about the ability of staff to accomplish substantial things (p. 56)

In this context, Marzano and colleagues discuss the role of school leaders in developing *collective efficacy,* which is defined as "group members' shared perception or belief that they can dramatically enhance the effectiveness of their organization . . . the shared belief that 'we can make a difference'" (p. 99). They cite the research of Goddard, Hoy, and Hoy, who found that "the collective efficacy of the teachers in a school is a better predictor of student success in schools than is the socioeconomic status of the students" (p. 99). Note that efficacy appears in Dimensions 1 and 2 of Figure 3.1.

One of the five practices that Kouzes and Posner (2002) associate with effective leadership is enabling others to act. This practice is closely associated with the leadership function of maximizing. In *The Leadership Challenge,* they identify two primary behaviors related to this practice: fostering collaboration and strengthening others. Regarding strengthening others, they suggest that effective leaders "generate power all around." Here's what they say,

Exemplary leaders make other people feel strong. They enable others to take ownership of and responsibility for their group's success by enhancing their competence and confidence in their abilities, by listening to their ideas and acting upon them, by involving them in important decisions, and by acknowledging and giving credit for their contributions. Long before empowerment was written into the popular vocabulary, exemplary leaders understood how important it was that their constituents feel strong, capable, and efficacious. (p. 281)

This is maximizing—generating power all around. It is noteworthy that Kouzes and Posner view fostering collaboration to be a necessary companion to strengthening others. It is through the building of individual effectiveness in a collaborative work environment that leaders can nurture the collective efficacy that has been found to be so powerful in school settings. The maximizing leader's mental model (Figure 3.1) acknowledges the collective responsibility, collaborative culture, and knowledge and skill development identified by these two authorities on leadership.

Kouzes and Posner associate the asking of questions with the strengthening of individuals. They state,

> Questions develop people. They help others escape the trap of their own paradigms by broadening their perspectives and taking responsibility for their own viewpoints. . . . Another byproduct of asking other people for their ideas and listening to their suggestions is that such actions enhance self-worth. (p. 101)

These leadership experts suggest that questioning is a way of building trust within an organization because the posing of questions honors individuals' thinking and opinions. This takes us back to Hank and Magnolia Middle School:

Hank knew that he could not mandate that his faculty demonstrate collective efficacy and assume collective responsibility. They would need to come to this realization and commitment one by one. He did believe that he could facilitate their thinking about efficacy and responsibility by posing questions that would help them "escape the trap of their own paradigms."

Hank decided to dedicate two hours of one of the scheduled preschool professional development days to beginning this conversation with the faculty. He remembered a structured group process that he had experienced in a recent professional development session. Called Data on Display (see Resource B), this activity is a three-step process that begins with individual reflection and rating, moves to the creation of bar graphs on wall charts that represent the group's thinking, and culminates with community dialogue that emerges from an analysis of the data displayed on the charts. Hank began by developing five statements for individual rating:

1. *I believe that all students can learn.*
2. *Every student in our school is learning every day.*
3. *Each student is individually responsible for his or her own learning and achievement.*
4. *If their parents are not involved and supportive of their school and learning, students will not reach their potential.*
5. *As a teacher, I'm primarily responsible for the learning of my students. It's my job to ensure that each of my students meets high standards every day.*

Hank prepared a response sheet with the following directions: To what extent do you agree with each of the following statements? Indicate your rating, from 0 to 100%, on the continuum beneath each statement. When you have completed your ratings, use one of the small sticky notes to record your ratings on the wall charts.

Prior to the scheduled session, Hank prepared and posted wall charts in the meeting room, which was set with round tables—five chairs per table—to facilitate small-group dialogue. Hank opened the session by sharing the norms for communication that he had introduced to the faculty the previous year (see Chapter 2). He then refocused on the school's vision:

Students and adults learning every day in a school where everyone's talents are tapped and celebrated.

Hank shared the disaggregated results of the state assessment and asked each table group to discuss the data and develop one possible conclusion based on the data. When he asked each table to report out to the larger group, he found that the conclusions across the room were similar and on target: "Most students at Magnolia are doing okay, but one subgroup is performing abysmally." "The lower-SES students are not achieving at the same levels as the rest of the student body." "We seem to be failing some of our students." "It appears that one set of students is on the road to dropping out." While each table group said it differently, all acknowledged the achievement gap. After some dialogue across the groups, Hank indicated that this was the context in which he hoped they could reflect together for the remainder of the session. He then distributed the rating sheets and reviewed instructions with the group. He underscored the importance of everyone being completely honest and candid in their responses. Each person in the room individually completed a rating sheet and used sticky notes to display their ratings on wall charts.

The collective data displayed on the completed wall charts told a compelling story. Almost every staff member indicated a strong belief that all students can learn (Item 1); however, there was a wide range of responses to Item 2 ("Every student in our school is learning every day"), ranging from 30% to 90% agreement, with the mean response hovering around 60%. And responses to Items 3, 4, and 5 were literally "all over the map." The majority of staff rated student and parent responsibility at 60% or higher. The range of responses to the final item ("It's my job . . .") was 20% to 100%.

Hank posed the following question to the large group: "What do the data tell us?" One of the teachers, Rhonda, said, "There seems to be a discrepancy between what we believe and what we do." Hank silently agreed with Rhonda, but waited five seconds. Before he spoke to affirm Rhonda's response, she added, "Well, look at the difference in our ratings of items 1 and 2." Again, Hank waited. Tom, a teacher from another group spoke up: "Well, we were talking about the pattern of responses to Items 3 to 5. There appears to be a wide range of opinions in our group as to who is ultimately responsible for student learning." Hank waited, and there was complete silence. After eight seconds or so, Hank replied, "I agree with you. There is a lot of diversity in our thinking about this issue. Why do you think this is the case?" Again, there was stone silence. Hank was not flustered. He refocused the question. "Let's look at Item 3. I'd like to get behind the thinking of some of you who rated this item 80% or higher." The dialogue was off and running. Teachers shared their views on this and the remaining items. The conversation was rich. Speakers kept going back to the wall charts—posing additional questions and looking for contradictions. Hank could feel the energy in the room and was particularly pleased that almost everyone seemed very engaged. Toward the end of the session, a veteran teacher named Carolyn posed a question that caused everyone to sit up and take pause: "What would it take," she asked, "for each one of us to become convinced that 'it is our job, and we can do it?'" MaryJo, a third-grade teacher, responded, "I'm not sure I can buy that; we've got to have partnerships with students and parents if we are to be successful." "So," said Carolyn, "what would that look like? And isn't it our job to reach out and try to create these partnerships?"

Hank had to call the conversation to a halt when the allocated time for the session came to an end. He thanked faculty members for their openness and told them he wanted to keep the conversation alive. Someone suggested that he post follow-up questions on the walls of the teachers' planning area with the invitation to individuals and groups to post alternative responses. Hank agreed and asked if the teachers would like to come back in two weeks with these interim responses and continue the conversation. Most said, "Yes!" Hank emphasized that this would be a voluntary session. His head was spinning as he thought of other strategies for keeping the reflection and dialogue going while moving the group to action steps. The process had only begun, but Hank was confirmed in his belief that his faculty wanted to do all that they could for each student. It was his job to unleash the potential of this amazing group.

Faculty members at Magnolia Middle School are continuing to reinvent themselves and their school through individual reflection and group dialogue. Hank's leadership was a catalyst for changing the talk at this school. Out of these conversations emerged the teacher-identified need for increased knowledge and skills in differentiating instruction and using classroom management strategies to support differentiation. Hank met with grade-level team chairs to plan for this professional learning focus. They recommended a job-embedded approach utilizing teacher inquiry as the engine to drive the learning. Teacher leaders are using quality questioning to sustain ongoing learning in this area.

What lessons about quality questioning can we learn from Hank's story? Like any good open-ended question, there are multiple, correct responses to this one. We invite you to answer this question for yourself before reading our response.

Here's what *we* learned from our colleague Hank.

- Good structures support individual and group reflection.
- People need to make their own meaning from data. The same data mean different things to different individuals—depending on their worldview.
- When individuals are given the time, space, and encouragement to think, they usually will grapple with the hard issues.
- Quality questions demonstrate respect for differing perspectives.
- Quality questions build ownership.

EXAMPLES OF QUALITY QUESTIONS FOR MAXIMIZING PERFORMANCE

Quality Questions for Encouraging Individuals to Grow and Learn, Personally and Professionally

1. What did you learn from this experience?

2. What evidence can you collect to determine the impact of this new strategy on student learning?

3. If you could start this project anew, what would you do differently?

4. Is there someone on the faculty with whom you'd be willing to develop a "critical friend" relationship?

Quality Questions for Encouraging an Individual to Work Toward Organizational Goals

1. What kind of support would it take to enable you to achieve this goal?

2. What kinds of questions do you have about "the end we have in mind?"

3. In what ways does this goal align with your own values and aspirations?

4. Imagine what it would feel like to have all of your students actively engaged in learning. Think aloud about what you are doing when this is happening.

Quality Questions for Building Collective Will to Meet Challenges

1. What can we do to support one another in our quest to become a school of excellence?

2. What are our collective and individual strengths? In what ways can we build upon one another's individual strengths?

3. How will we know that we are on the right track—that we are improving our skills and effectiveness in this area?

4. What can we do to celebrate milestones along the way?

4

Mobilizing

How Do Leaders Build Constituent Commitment to Act?

Purpose is a unique source of energy and power. . . . Purpose becomes a more powerful and enduring source of energy in our lives in three ways: when its source moves from negative to positive, external to internal and self to others.

—Jim Loehr and Tony Schwartz, *The Power of Full Engagement*

FOCUS QUESTIONS

1. What outcomes result when leaders are strategic in their efforts to mobilize individual and collective energy around a goal or purpose?

2. Why is clarification of purpose an important lever in the development of individual commitment?

3. What is the role of questioning in the activation of individual and collective commitment to an organizational purpose?

4. What kinds of structures and designs do leaders use to engage colleagues in conversations that will promote collective ownership and action?

Janet is Assistant Superintendent for Instruction in Green Valley, a small, progressive school district. She knows that good things are happening in the nine schools in her district. She is not certain, however, that school and district leaders share a compelling vision for teaching and learning in the 21st century, nor is she convinced that good practices in one school are being shared with all other schools across the district. She believes that a districtwide learning collaborative, to include the principal and another instructional leader from each school as well as central office staff, can support this "very good" district's movement to "great." She thinks that an inquiry approach to the work of the proposed collaborative can reenergize and mobilize leaders and their staffs around the district's vision of excellence in teaching and learning.

Mobilizing is the process of getting people on board, of motivating them to act. Sometimes the challenge is to mobilize individuals to accept a new mandate or program. More often, it's to mobilize people to meet high expectations day in and day out in their work, as is the case at Green Valley School District. Action, activity, collaboration—all of these require human energy. Loehr and Schwartz (2003) are among those who tie personal and organizational excellence to the effective management of energy. The goal is to create "high positive" energy across the organization. According to these authors, this occurs when individuals are "invigorated, confident, challenged, joyful, and connected" (p. 10). As stated in the quote above, purpose is the key to energy and power.

In *The Answer to How Is Yes*, Peter Block (2003) makes a compelling case for greater focus on purpose. Block argues that organizations too often overlook purpose in favor of immediate action. He says the premature asking of the *how* question is a trap into which most of us fall. He identifies six such questions: *How do you do it? How long will it take? How much does it cost? How do you get those people to change? How do we measure it? How are other people doing it successfully?* (pp. 34–36). Block argues that these questions sometimes express our doubts about our ability to pursue a certain pathway, not our curiosity. *How* questions can be roadblocks to action if posed too early in the problem-solving process. It's not that such questions are bad; in fact, they are necessary, productive, and can lead to precipitous action—if asked at the appropriate juncture. The time to ask *how* questions is *after* questions pertaining to purpose, intent, rationale, and alternatives have been discussed and answered. Block believes that we tend to "prefer action and answers to thinking and questioning" (p. 75). Ironically, this preference for action can keep us from achieving our goal. To borrow an analogy from Stephen R. Covey (1990), if we don't take the time to make sure our ladder is leaning against the right wall before we take action, every step simply gets us to the wrong place faster.

Michael Fullan (2007) is also a strong advocate of attending to purpose. He elaborates on contrasting problems found in school organizations and leadership: the "too-loose" problem and the "too-tight" solution. He defines the too-loose problem as one for which constituents lack focus and clarity. Directly addressing such a problem with "standards-based reform gets us into the dysfunctions of the 'too-tight' solution" (p. 29). Because people are unable to see a connection between the problem and the solution, they become frustrated and feel powerless. Fullan holds that the solution is to create "infrastructures and processes" that allow individuals to discover "deep meaning about new approaches to teaching and learning" (p. 29). Quality questions are requisite to such meaning finding.

Like Fullan, Peter Senge (1990) connects meaning seeking with consequential planning and coordinated action and holds that well-formulated questions are vehicles that drive the meaning-making function in organizations. Only when individuals have the opportunity to find meaning in a proposed plan of action do they develop a deep, internal commitment that will not only move them to action but also sustain their course over time. Let's see how these ideas play out in Janet's district.

As Janet reflected upon the challenge of taking Green Valley schools to the next level, she contemplated the power of purpose, processes, and infrastructures. She believed that leaders needed a common vision of 21st-century teaching and learning. Her background reading and research had made her aware that a number of visions related to 21st-century teaching and learning had been crafted by national organizations. In fact, she knew that the leadership in a neighboring district had adopted a related vision three or four years ago. While the vision was sound, few people in that district understood or owned it. (This is an example of a too-tight solution.) *Green Valley had not addressed the 21st-century learning issues as a district in the early days of the movement; rather, the superintendent and her leadership team had decided to allow each school to create its own pathway to more powerful learning. And, predictably, there was not coherence across the district.* (This is an example of a too-loose approach.) *So, Janet and the superintendent decided to create a districtwide collaborative to focus on the most important business of the district. They communicated with principals to develop a schedule for meetings that would work for building-level leaders.*

The districtwide learning collaborative, which would convene every four to six weeks, was a new infrastructure for the Green Valley school system. Janet knew that the kick-off session would set the tone for the initiative. She and the superintendent talked about the purpose of the collaborative and agreed that it was to mobilize the district's leadership around a shared vision for successful teaching and learning in an ever-changing global society and to provide these leaders with the skills and processes that would enable them to similarly mobilize their schools' professional learning communities. Janet and members of the design team wrestled with questions of purpose: What outcomes are we attempting to create in the initial session? What end do we have in mind? After considerable reflection, team members agreed that they would like to (1) engage leaders in forging a shared vision for teaching and learning and a shared understanding of a professional learning community through which teacher learning and planning occur and (2) establish dialogue as a way of conversing during the collaborative sessions. The team chose a structured group process called Ink Think (included in Resource B) as the opening activity. This activity was designed to promote both content and process objectives.

Ink Think begins with individual reflection, during which all participants respond silently to a set of focus questions. Following individual reflection, each participant takes a felt-tip marker and moves to a wall chart, where colleagues work together to create a collective response to one of the focus questions. The protocol for the activity requires participants to communicate by writing on the chart. Their charge is to create a concept map charting their ideas, so they must "listen with their eyes" to what others in their group contribute. They are encouraged to piggyback on others' thoughts and to establish new categories of concepts as appropriate. Janet and her team had crafted the following four questions and printed them on a handout for each participant.

1. *What does "21st-century teaching and learning" mean to you? What would you expect to see in a school that embraces this vision?*

2. *How would you define or describe a professional learning community? What would you expect to see and hear in a school that embraces this way of "doing business?"*

3. *If visitors came to Green Valley schools to see good examples of 21st-century teaching and learning, what would you show them? What initiatives and best practices would you point to?*

4. *What challenges and barriers do you confront, as district and school leaders, in your efforts to advance 21st-century teaching and learning?*

As the session facilitator, Janet allocated eight minutes for individual reading and initial response to all four questions. The 24 participants were seated 6 to a table. Following individual reflection, Janet assigned one of the questions to each table group and asked each table to take the markers provided and move to the wall chart designated for their question. There, group members silently charted their ideas during the six minutes of allocated time. (Members of each table team received markers of the same color and were asked to use this color throughout the activity.) At the end of this stage, Janet asked each group to move clockwise to the next wall chart—taking their markers with them—and to review what the previous group had recorded in response to its question. During the review, participants placed checkmarks beside those ideas with which they agreed. They used the remainder of the six-minute block of time to add their own ideas to the concept map. Groups made three rotations so that everyone in the room was able to record responses to all four questions. Finally, Janet instructed the groups to move back to their beginning station. Until this point, everyone had been instructed to work silently. Janet told them they could now talk aloud about their question and the sets of responses that had been added to their wall chart by other groups. They were instructed to cluster like ideas together and to identify four to six major themes. There was a buzz of talk as teams reacted to the group products.

Team reports revealed a rich tapestry of responses. As the major themes were reported, leaders noticed consistent patterns in the responses. During the debrief, individuals remarked on the power of the process to engage everyone over the duration of the activity, on the interactions that had occurred silently, on the opportunity for everyone's voice to be heard, and on the amount of information that was brought to the fore in a relatively short amount of time. School leaders indicated they would like to repeat the process with their entire faculties.

The school leaders' remarks were a natural lead-in to Janet's introduction of dialogue. She presented a synthesis of thinking about this mode of conversation, which is characterized by four critical elements that are related to quality questioning: (1) listening, (2) respecting, (3) suspending judgment, and (4) voicing. Janet distributed a Dialogue Tool (see Figure 4.1) to all participants, asking them to review the tool with an "elbow partner" and to think together about how their experience with Ink Think provided silent practice in the use of dialogue. As Janet processed the talk by partners, consensus emerged that the Ink Think activity had been important practice in the four critical elements of dialogue. Janet listened to the excitement in the room and felt the session was moving toward attainment of the hoped-for outcomes. She told the group that the last activity of the session would give them an opportunity to practice dialogue in the more traditional, verbal manner.

In dialogue we listen, seek to understand, hold our assumptions in the air of critique. We do not seek decisions, actions, or justifications. The promise of dialogue is that we may invent visions of what could be in our schools and organizations.

—Linda Lambert (2002, p. 71)

Participants at each table received one of four excerpts from current thought leaders related to 21st-century teaching and learning. Janet asked individuals to read their excerpt and talk about what, if anything, they might add to the concept maps based on their understanding of the author's perspective—and to say which of the group's ideas were confirmed by this author. The excerpts sparked new ideas for each of the concept maps. All groups used black felt-tip markers to distinguish thought leaders' ideas from their own as they added additional insights to the concept maps.

As the session came to a close, participants completed an assessment form that asked them to rate the extent to which they and their colleagues had honored the four critical elements of dialogue (listening, respecting, suspending judgment, and voicing) during their interactions in the session. Self-assessments were positive, but participants agreed that they needed more practice—especially in the verbal (as opposed to the nonverbal) mode!

Figure 4.1	A Dialogue Tool

Critical Element and Questions for Reflection	Positive Indicators: Evidence of Use	Negative Indicators: Evidence of Forgetfulness
LISTENING		
Are you listening to self? Are you focusing on what the speaker is saying and keeping your own thoughts in the background? Are you monitoring your listening to minimize judgments, doubts, and rebuttals? *Are you open to other perspectives?* Are you listening from a position of neutrality and detachment, with a willingness to consider all perspectives? Are you willing to be influenced by what others say? *Are you listening for collective meaning?* Are you listening for patterns and collective themes? Are you listening for interrelationships among all perspectives?	Giving nonverbal messages that say "I'm listening" (e.g., focusing on the speaker, making eye contact with the speaker) Being silent after a speaker stops talking Acknowledging what other speakers have said; building upon another's ideas Asking questions to clarify or expand understanding of the speaker's ideas	Interrupting the speaker Judging or evaluating the speaker's comment Offering a rebuttal to the speaker's comments Demonstrating impatience (e.g., fidgeting, repeatedly checking a watch or clock) Holding fast to a preconceived idea Advocating for your own position
RESPECTING		
Are you actively recognizing and valuing everyone else at the table? Are you listening to understand other perspectives?	Asking a question about another's perspective Encouraging a speaker to continue talking or to provide more information	Interrupting another Ignoring another's contribution (i.e., speaking after another without regard to what he or she may have said)

Critical Element and Questions for Reflection	Positive Indicators: Evidence of Use	Negative Indicators: Evidence of Forgetfulness
	Referring to a point that another speaker made earlier	Contradicting another speaker
		Failing to make eye contact
	Adding to or elaborating on another's comment	
		Using nonverbal putdowns (e.g., eye-rolling, shoulder shrugging)
	Appreciating or acknowledging another's comment, perhaps by just repeating it	

SUSPENDING JUDGMENT

Critical Element and Questions for Reflection	Positive Indicators: Evidence of Use	Negative Indicators: Evidence of Forgetfulness
Are you speaking openly and honestly?	Asking questions to get behind another's thinking	Speaking down to another or using a patronizing tone of voice
Are you inquiring into others' positions?	Seeking clarification of language or the meaning of words	Making assumptions about what someone else intended or meant
Do you take care not to advocate for your or any one else's position?	Identifying relationships or connections between various speakers' ideas	Advocating for your own or another's position
Do you refrain from making value judgments?	Asking for time out to think or reflect on what's been said	Making value judgments
Are you listening for connections between and among different speakers' ideas?		Trying to problem solve or reach consensus or closure (prematurely)
		Demonstrating certitude

VOICING

Critical Element and Questions for Reflection	Positive Indicators: Evidence of Use	Negative Indicators: Evidence of Forgetfulness
Are you seeking or searching for unspoken ideas or questions?	Asking: ○ What are we ignoring or leaving out of this conversation? ○ What are we failing to pay attention to?	Blabbering (i.e., speaking without purpose or forethought)
Are you speaking the truth?		Monopolizing the conversation

(Continued)

| Figure 4.1 | (Continued) |

Critical Element and Questions for Reflection	Positive Indicators: Evidence of Use	Negative Indicators: Evidence of Forgetfulness
Are you giving voice to what may be new or uncomfortable ideas for you? Are you giving yourself permission to say what is on your mind—without self-censorship?	Choosing one's words carefully	Seeking reinforcement or agreement from others
	Monitoring one's talk—not speaking without thinking	Moving to a "comfortable" position in an effort to reach a compromise or consensus
	Asking hard questions	Seeking unanimity
	Challenging a long-held, perhaps implicit, assumption	Filling the silence with talk
	Taking a risk by articulating what may be outside-of-the-box thinking	
	Demonstrating a willingness to be inconsistent in one's thinking and speaking	
	Honoring the silence	

Source: Jackie A. Walsh, Alabama Best Practices Center.

Peter Senge and colleagues (1999) distinguish between compliance and commitment, the two forces that work to mobilize individuals to action in organizations. They conclude that "deep changes—in how people think, what they believe, how they see the world—are difficult, if not impossible, to achieve through compliance" (p. 13). Learning is always embedded in profound change, which "combines *inner shifts* in people's values, aspirations, and behaviors with *outer shifts* in processes, strategies, practices, and systems" (p. 15). Green Valley School District seeks to build individual and collective commitment for the things that matter most: teaching and learning. District leaders understand and model the importance of facilitating the individual creation of meaning through reflection—and the collective creation of meaning through public reflection, skillful discussion, and dialogue. The district learning collaborative provides time and space for this reflection and dialogue.

When leaders arrived for the second session of the Green Valley's district learning collaborative, they came with reports of how they used their learnings from the first session in their schools. Participants revisited their work products from the first session, and Janet used processes for the second session to move the dialogue forward.

We have reported only the beginning phase of the Green Valley School District leadership's work to mobilize all Green Valley schools to adopt best practices and provide cutting-edge teaching and learning for all students. At last report, the initiative continued, and the district collaborative was being institutionalized.

The story of Green Valley exemplifies the role that quality questioning can play in mobilizing leaders across a district in support of a coherent, powerful vision for teaching and learning. Fullan (2007) argues that most initiatives flounder and lose steam because leaders fail to help members of the school community make personal meaning of the change. In Fullan's view, the process of making meaning is a powerful catalyst for individual and collective motivation. Individuals are motivated when they have the opportunity to develop a clear understanding of what they are being asked to do and when they find personal meaning in the course of developing this understanding.

EXAMPLES OF QUALITY QUESTIONS FOR
MOBILIZING GROUPS AND INDIVIDUALS

1. Let's begin with the end in mind. What difference will it make for our students if we are able to accomplish this?

2. What can you contribute to make this initiative effective?

3. What do you believe to be our primary purpose for adopting this initiative?

4. Why do you think we should pursue this course?

5. In what ways do the elements of this program align with our core values?

6. What are we trying to create together?

7. What matters most to you? Which one of these alternatives best matches that value?

8. What is one thing that you'd be willing to do tomorrow to get this process rolling?

9. Who can you work with to develop these ideas?

10. What can you stop doing so that you can be a part of this team?

11. Create an alternative to this design—one that will work in our school.

5

Mediating

How Does Quality Questioning Help Create Common Ground?

There are three ways of dealing with difference: domination, compromise, and integration. By domination only one side gets what it wants; by compromise neither side gets what it wants; by integration we find a way by which both sides may get what they wish.

—Mary Parker Follett, *Wisdom Quotes*

FOCUS QUESTIONS

1. What outcomes result when leaders use questions to understand and manage conflict among members of their community?

2. In what ways can leaders use questioning to surface differences and encourage respect of divergent thinking?

3. What kinds of questions can we use to mediate understanding of complex and potentially controversial issues?

4. How can we use each of the four elements of quality questioning to mediate and resolve conflict?

How Can Leaders Use Quality Questioning to Resolve Conflict?

James Howard, the principal at Watson High School, answered the phone and heard the irate voice of Mrs. Irene Johnson, the parent of a student leader. Mrs. Johnson was obviously in distress. "That new science teacher, Mrs. Sylvester, is ruining my child's life!" she said. "J. T. hates school because of her, and I want to know what you are going to do about it." James listened thoughtfully and respectfully. He took a deep breath and counted silently to three after Mrs. Johnson stopped speaking. He calmly told her he'd like to learn more about the situation and then have a conference. (See Resource B, Interview or Conference.) "We'll include Mrs. Sylvester in the conference; we want to understand your point of view, and we'll want to understand hers as well. Should we include J. T. since this is about him?" James asked. "Well, I'd rather not at this point; if we need to involve him later, I'm more than happy for that to happen," responded Mrs. Johnson. James scheduled the meeting for three days hence, giving himself adequate time to gather more information and develop a plan.

James wandered down to Mrs. Sylvester's classroom during her planning period. "I got a call from J. T.'s mother. She seems to think that he has developed a bad attitude toward school. What have you noticed about J. T. recently?" Mrs. Sylvester, a first-year teacher, seemed unsure of herself. "Well, he does all of his assignments and even some optional work assignments." James continued, "His mother thinks it may have something to do with your class. I've invited her in for a conference with you and me. What can you tell me about J. T.'s performance in your class?" Things had been going pretty well, she thought, and she couldn't remember anything negative about the young man in her class. "He seems very interested. He's always asking questions. Sometimes we don't have time for his questions, because in science there are so many state standards to cover." She paused, "Mr. Howard, I'm so sorry for causing a problem. I can't imagine what this might be about." James assured her they would work as a team—principal, parent, and teacher— to figure this out. "No apologies are needed. When you come to the conference, bring your grade book, some samples of his work, and recent assignments. Also, between now and then, you might want to do some reflection and see if anything comes to mind."

Clearly, thought James, this is a situation where there are different perceptions. This will be interesting; it will require some skillful listening and probing to better understand what's happening before we can get to the bottom of this one.

Mediating is an important leadership function in a school, as in any organization, especially if the leader is working to create a learning community with shared leadership and responsibility. In a culture where mediation is the norm, individuals work to resolve their misunderstandings with the assistance of another party. In this type of culture, leaders expect and support individuals in working through a process that leads to enhanced understanding of the other's point of view and to an eventual resolution of the issue. Leaders do not assume the authoritarian (and paternalistic) role of judging who is "right" or "wrong" in conflicts. Although there are certainly occasions when the principal or other key leader will have to become the final arbiter of a disagreement, this should be a fall-back position taken only when other measures have failed.

> *Conflict is neither positive nor negative in and of itself. . . . Each of us has influence and power over whether or not conflict becomes negative, and that influence and power is found in the way we handle it.*
>
> —Dudley Weeks (1992, p. 7)

Educators tend to avoid conflict, says Robert Evans (1996) in *The Human Side of School Change: Reform, Resistance, and the Real-Life Problems of Innovation*. "School leaders generally prefer to minimize friction and discord, overlooking them when they can, finessing and fudging them when they can't," he writes. Many administrators, on finding themselves in the situation of principal James Howard, would have the goal of settling down or appeasing the parent without escalating the issue; others would want to protect the teacher—and the school—at all costs. In our scenario, James had a different goal. He wanted to help J. T. thrive; clearly, according to his mother, something was interfering with J. T. in his role as learner and student. James understood the value of listening to diverse points of view as a way to improve his understanding of others. He tended to see conflict as healthy and wanted to help a first-year teacher see the potential in learning through conflicts that arise from diverse points of view.

The most important role that a leader can take in mediating misunderstandings is that of information seeker, listener, and questioner. Roger Soder (2001) offers five basic principles that relate to leaders' discharge of the information-seeking role:

1. Many people will tell you what they think you want to hear.

2. People often won't tell you the truth because they don't want to compromise themselves.

3. The power of the leader can get in the way of getting people to tell the truth.

4. Leaders must be aware of the dangers of optimism and preconceived ideas.

5. How you go about seeking information speaks to your character. (pp. 31–38)

These five principles can apply to any situation in which leaders are seeking information, but their impact on leader effectiveness when mediating is particularly critical.

Soder's first three principles speak to the importance of establishing a climate of trust. It is particularly important that individuals in conflict trust the communications process in which they are engaging. Dennis and Michelle Reina (2006) define *communications trust* as "the willingness to share information, tell the truth, admit mistakes, maintain confidentiality, give and receive constructive feedback, and speak with good purpose" (p. 34). Fear is an obvious barrier to communications trust, and fear does not disappear from a culture just because we wish it away. Traditionally, schools have had a very hierarchical power structure and used autocratic methods for conflict resolution. In practice, this meant that teachers had the power to make decisions about conflicts between and among students—and administrators had the ultimate decision-making power in all conflicts. Hence, leaders must work overtime to establish a climate where truth telling is valued. In the words of the Reinas, "Trust develops when people feel comfortable and safe enough to share their perceptions regarding one another's perceptions without repercussions. They trust they will not suffer the consequences of retaliation because they spoke the truth" (p. 47).

When leaders assume the mediator role, they need to maintain a third-party, objective point of view. Soder warns against taking preconceptions to the process—especially if these are assumptions about either party engaged in the dispute. Not only does the mediator need to be nonjudgmental with regard to the personalities involved, he or she also needs to guard against preconceived notions about specific outcomes. The most important skills in effective mediating are active listening and quality questioning.

James was aware of the need to cement a trusting relationship with Mrs. Sylvester, whose teaching position at Watson High School was the first of her career. James was known as an open-minded and fair administrator; however, he realized that first-year teachers are aiming to please. He wanted to be sure that Mrs. Sylvester would be comfortable reflecting honestly and openly. He also was aware of his predisposition to favor J. T., a likable student with whom he had a positive relationship. He was determined to stay neutral, supportive, and open.

The next day, James dropped by to see Mrs. Sylvester. They talked informally to establish rapport. Because she seemed worried—and, he thought, a bit frightened about the conference—he said, "You know, Mrs. Sylvester, each of us sees the world through our own lens. At the conference with Mrs. Johnson, our job will be to listen in order to understand her point of view. We don't have to agree; we don't have to disagree. We'll try to listen with an open mind. Even if she makes accusations, we'll try not to be reactive, but rather seek to understand where she's coming from. It's only through listening respectfully that we'll be able to understand—and eventually solve—this problem. My belief is that if we keep an open mind and stay calm we'll learn something that can help this school become a better place for students to learn. I want you to know, this is not about assigning blame, but rather about identifying and correcting a problem."

The principal believed in the benefits of planning. He also believed that all parties involved in the current situation shared a common purpose: helping J. T. learn to the best of his ability and develop to his fullest potential. He decided he would begin the conference with a statement to that effect and pose a question that would help Mrs. Johnson be specific in stating the problem from her perspective. He worked to formulate his opening question.

- *"What concerns do you have about J. T.?" wasn't specific enough.*
- *"What makes you think J. T. hates school?" or "Why are you concerned about your son? What has he said or done to indicate he doesn't like school?" might cause her to become defensive—to think the school was questioning her perceptiveness as a mother.*
- *"When we talked on the phone, you indicated that J. T. doesn't like school. Can you help us understand what led you to this conclusion?" This might be the question to begin with.*

The principal thought about where he could meet with the parent. His office was not neutral ground; it carried the symbol of his authority. Mrs. Sylvester's classroom gave her a psychological advantage. He decided to meet in the counselor's conference room, where all parties would be more comfortable.

On the day of the conference, James began by welcoming both parent and teacher and establishing some ground rules for the meeting. "What we want to do is come to an understanding so that we can help J. T. be the best student he can be. We believe that all of us can contribute to that understanding. And listening is the first priority. Let's try this, if you're willing. One of us will speak. Before the next person speaks, he or she will summarize what the previous speaker said and wait for confirmation or clarification before proceeding with another comment. Will that work for you both?" As both parent and teacher nodded, he continued with his prepared question: "Mrs. Johnson, when we talked on the phone, you indicated that J. T. doesn't like school. Can you help us understand what led you to this conclusion?"

Mrs. Johnson's answer to his initial question surprised him. J. T. had come home from school and thrown down his book bag, exclaiming, "I'd like to quit school." As his mother probed, she learned that in science class that day, Mrs. Sylvester had said, "J. T., you've got one more question to ask today, so you'd better make it good!" J. T. had been embarrassed by the attention this brought him; in addition, he felt that his questions were not valued. "What's the use of going to school if it's not to learn?" he'd wailed at his mother. Mrs. Johnson avoided looking at the teacher and said directly to James, "So. Is that the way you expect your teachers to respond to students who are curious? I want to know what you plan to do about this situation."

James didn't respond immediately. In the pause that followed, Mrs. Sylvester spoke. She rephrased what she had heard the parent say, received a confirmation, and then said, "I remember that day. I'll be honest, that was not my best day. I was expecting an observation from central office and I was on edge." She continued, "I always saw J. T. as a confident student; I never gave a second thought to the impact of my statement."

James summarized her comment and asked, "I'm wondering what the two of you think we should do?"

The teacher said, "I don't want to stifle any student's thinking. I need to talk to J. T. and apologize." Mrs. Johnson added, "Well, I can certainly explain to J. T. that everyone has good and bad days, and sometimes we take things personally when they are not intended to be." After a pause, she looked at Mrs. Sylvester and asked, "But I want to know, was it unintended? Or do you prefer that students not ask questions?"

Mrs. Sylvester quickly responded, "Oh, I think questions show interest. They are good." Then she equivocated, "But you know, sometimes it takes a lot more time when students ask questions; we have so much to cover in that class."

There was another long pause. Mrs. Johnson looked unhappy. James intervened, "I think this is a good topic to consider at our next team meeting. When I do walk-throughs, I hear very few student questions. I know that teachers are working hard to help students learn all the material. But, I believe questioning is an important tool for student learning. I believe, like you, Mrs. Sylvester, that student questions show interest and understanding. I'd really like for our school to take on the challenge of helping students and teachers develop an understanding of how powerful a question can be. What do the two of you think of making that the focus for professional learning here at our school?"

Dialogue helps us suspend judgment and introduce more inquiry and listening into the conversation. Our objective is to open the door for more innovative alternatives to emerge.

—Linda Ellinor and Glenda Gerard (1998, p. 200)

We acknowledge that not all conflict can be mediated to such a positive resolution. But, the scenario demonstrates that leaders who have mastered quality questioning are better at managing conflict because they possess the skills necessary to encourage open communication and get to the true cause of the conflict. Paul Preuss (2003) refers to the core problem as the root cause and defines it as "the deepest underlying cause, or causes, of positive or negative symptoms within any process that, if dissolved, would result in elimination, or substantial reduction, of the symptom" (p. 3). Getting to the root cause of a conflict is the key to successful mediation. Unfortunately, because mediation is sometimes uncomfortable, leaders are often quick to latch on to the first potential cause of the conflict that is uncovered in order to end the process as quickly as possible. This rush to a conclusion more often than not results in a surface understanding of the problem. In such instances, symptoms are often treated while the real cause of the conflict is allowed to continue festering. Such half-hearted attempts at mediation fail to solve problems and are an unwise use of resources such as time, personnel, and goodwill. Leaders who use questions effectively in the mediation process, however, are providing a clear indication that they value the views of all parties and are seeking to surface the root causes of the conflict, paving the way for successful conflict resolution.

How Can Leaders Mediate Understanding of Complex and Potentially Controversial Issues?

Listening and questioning for understanding is essential to mediation. These mediation skills are a starting point for education leaders who wish to help others move their thinking to increasingly higher levels. Doing so can build a school community's capacity to address complex issues. Consider, for example, the following scenario:

> *Meg Walton, the principal of MLK Elementary School, had noticed that teachers in her school had very different approaches to assigning grades to students. Letter grade values were specified by the district: 93–100 = A, and so forth. But, the way teachers arrived at numeric grade averages varied widely. Some teachers deducted points for neatness; others for incorrect headings. Some teachers asked students to grade their own papers according to a predetermined rubric; others did not. Some teachers gave zeros for incomplete homework assignments; others allowed students to retake tests until they attained a passing grade. As far as Meg could tell, there was no consistency in practice. More than that, when she brought up the subject, she realized that teachers felt strongly about their ways of assigning grades. For sure, there was no common practice or shared understanding about grading; she saw this as an important topic for potential improvement.*

This scenario brings us to a second dimension of mediation—that of helping a group of people come to a shared understanding of an issue and, as a community of learners, develop new practices and principles. Leaders frequently are called upon to use the skills of mediation *before* conflict develops—especially concerning issues that are likely to trigger strong emotional reactions.

> *Meg knew the value of letting people voice their opinions and be heard. She wanted to use the issue of grading practices to help her faculty begin to develop the skills of dialogue, but she believed they needed some processes to scaffold these skills. And she knew that the school faculty needed to approach the topic slowly, without being told the right and wrong ways to think about it. Indeed, this seemed to provide an opportunity for true inquiry.*
>
> *As Meg prepared for the first session, she decided that she would use Interview Design (as described in Resource B) as a process for allowing everyone to be heard equitably and safely. She knew that, in this process, every teacher would be asked his or her opinion and would be heard by a partner—with no discussion. This would help to establish a nonthreatening environment in which teachers could voice their beliefs—and be prompted to reflect on their values, beliefs, and actions. Meg created four questions with the help of a lead teacher who was willing to work on the issue.*

Interview Design Questions

MLK Elementary School

Topic: Grading Practices

Question 1. In *Transforming Classroom Grading,* Marzano (2000) describes five common reasons for giving grades: "(1) for administrative purposes, (2) to give students feedback about their progress and achievement, (3) to provide guidance to students about future course work, (4) to provide guidance to teachers for instructional planning, and (5) to motivate students." (p. 14)

Rank these five purposes from most to least important. In considering the most important purpose, comment on how grades serve—or fail to serve—that function.

Question 2. In *Transforming Classroom Grading,* Marzano (2000) cites a 1996 study in which K–12 teachers were asked "to identify those skills and abilities *in addition* to subject-matter content that they consider when assigning grades to students" (p. 4). To varying degrees, teachers reported using the following factors in determining grades: academic performance, effort, behavior, cooperation, and attendance.

What factors do you consider when assigning a grade to student work? How do you assign weights to the various factors? Include such things as accuracy, length, neatness, format, and timeliness in addition to the factors identified by Marzano.

Question 3. The overall theme of *Transforming Classroom Grading* (Marzano, 2000) is that "a single letter grade or a percentage score is not a good way to report student achievement in any subject area because it simply cannot present the level of detailed feedback necessary for effective learning" (p. 106). A better alternative, he advocates, is standards-based grading, in which students are given information about achievement for each standard in a course.

What would be the benefits to adopting a standards-based approach to grading? Name at least three or four.

Question 4. The overall theme of *Transforming Classroom Grading* (Marzano, 2000) is that "a single letter grade or a percentage score is not a good way to report student achievement in any subject area because it simply cannot present the level of detailed feedback necessary for effective learning" (p. 106). A better alternative, he advocates, is standards-based grading, in which students are given information about achievement for each standard in a course.

What would be the challenges of adopting a standards-based approach to grading in this school? Name at least three or four.

When Meg conducted the Interview Design process, she was pleased to see that the teachers really enjoyed talking to each other about grading practices. The Interview Design process allowed one-to-one sharing on a subject that was rarely talked about. Meg could feel the energy in the room as the process of asking and answering questions was followed; it continued through the summarizing and reporting. She noticed that teachers hung around after the meeting was over that afternoon to continue their discussion and review of what others had said.

At the next meeting, Meg decided to take a larger risk. She prepared a prompt around which people would agree or disagree, and planned to use Peoplegraph (as described in Resource B) as a way to process differing points of view. As people gathered in the media center, she asked them to consider the following statement and to write their opinions. She read, "Some people have advocated eliminating zeroes from the grade books. Write for a few minutes about what the outcome may be if we were to adopt this policy." Meg allowed some time for teachers to write; she herself wrote about the topic during this time, modeling reflection. After allowing sufficient time, she said, "Now, think about what you wrote and where you stand on the issue of eliminating zeroes in grading. I've posted some phrases on the wall here indicating a range from Strongly Agree to Strongly Disagree. Stand along the continuum in the place that best describes your belief about the following statement: Teachers should eliminate zeroes from their grade books." A loud conversational buzz erupted as teachers moved to their places on the continuum. Meg noticed that teachers were all along the continuum; this would be a healthy discussion! She interrupted and gave directions: "Gather in groups of three or four with others who are standing near you. Choose a recorder to take notes. Talk together about why you chose to take the position you did."

Meg's strategies were but an opening for teachers to begin to reflect together and talk openly together. The teachers at MLK Elementary have continued by selecting several books to study; each teacher chose one of the books and joined a group that meets monthly to discuss it. The various groups then bring ideas back to the full community.

Both Meg and James gave particular attention to quality questioning by carefully crafting questions; selecting appropriate processes to engage all participants; establishing and modeling norms for openness and listening; and encouraging and scaffolding trust, respect, and thoughtfulness. True mediation is not about wins and losses; it is not about who holds fast to a position and who relents. True mediation creates common understanding and utilizes the best of both sides to create the most appropriate and positive outcome.

EXAMPLES OF QUALITY QUESTIONS FOR MEDIATING

**Quality Questions for Seeking to Help
Others Understand and Manage Conflict**

1. What would you like to occur as a result of this conversation?

2. Describe what happened (or what led up to this misunderstanding) in your own words.

3. What is your perception of the problem?

4. What might have happened to cause you to react in this way?

5. Why are we here? What is our purpose?

6. Let's think about what a "win-win" would look like.

7. What did you think it meant when he made that statement?

8. Help us understand how you felt when this happened.

9. If you could go back to the incident, what would you do differently?

10. Put yourself in the other party's position. Why do you think she may have acted as she did?

**Quality Questions for Attempting to Assist Others in Making
Meaning of Difficult and Potentially Controversial Issues**

1. What is your approach to this particular practice?

2. Can you generate alternative ways of approaching this particular issue?

3. What assumptions are you making?

4. What experiences have you had with this particular practice or program?

5. Can you identify what contributed to your way of thinking about this?

6. What concerns do you have about this potential change?

7. What is the worst thing that might happen if you accepted . . . ?

8. What do you think we mean when we say . . . ?

9. Identify ways in which this seems different from what you are currently doing.

6

Monitoring

How Do Leaders Use Quality Questioning to Facilitate Reflection on Progress Toward Identified Goals?

People need to know whether they're making progress towards the goal or simply marking time. Standards help to serve that function. But standards and goals are not enough. People's motivation to increase their productivity on a task increases only when they have a challenging goal and receive feedback on their progress.

—James Kouzes and Barry Posner, *The Leadership Challenge*

FOCUS QUESTIONS

1. What outcomes result when leaders are strategic in their efforts to facilitate collaborative progress monitoring?
2. Why is it important to emphasize self-assessment and lateral accountability in a monitoring system?
3. What are the characteristics of questions that engage individuals in effective progress monitoring?
4. What kinds of structures and processes can leaders employ to promote a school community's commitment to ongoing monitoring of performance?

Angela was a literacy coach in Westwood Elementary School. The staff had recently been involved in training to promote higher-level thinking. Staff had worked in teams to design higher-level questions and appropriate feedback to students. Despite what seemed like effective training, Angela had a nagging question: Were teachers using the tools they learned about to create higher-level questions for their students—and to prompt all students to think at higher levels? More important, Angela wondered, were students actually thinking more? And would these higher-level questions result in more learning and better comprehension in reading? Would it translate into higher achievement test scores?

In Angela's opinion, the focus on higher-level thinking was on target; she believed it had the potential to benefit the Westwood students and teachers with whom she worked. She wondered what the teachers thought about it, how they had used it, and with what results. She knew that as she observed, she saw a few more high-level questions; but she also knew that she was not the best person to assess the level or the effectiveness of the questions. That was surely for the teachers to decide.

At a team meeting, Angela introduced the idea of reflection and self-assessment. She explained a process called Reflective Questioning (as described in the Resource B) that she wanted to use with them. The teachers were willing to give it a try, so Angela distributed a two-column handout she had prepared in advance (see Figure 6.1).

Angela then asked teachers to reflect and respond individually to the prompt in the left-hand column. When they all seemed to be finished writing, she asked them to do the same for the prompt in the right-hand column. Then, utilizing the Reflective Questioning protocol, she asked them to form triads. Within each triad, one member served as an interviewer, one as a reflector/respondent, and one as an observer of the process. It was the observer's job to document verbal and nonverbal communication strategies that seemed to elicit the deepest and most reflective thinking.

As the teachers moved into triads and began talking, Angela was amazed at the depth of sharing. She moved around the group, listening unobtrusively, and heard a range of responses—from teachers who had had very little success to those who daily engaged students in thinking, taught their students about different levels of thinking, and provided scaffolds for students to formulate high-level responses. All teachers were engaged in listening or speaking; all seemed to be learning from one another; and, as Angela was pleased to note, they all seemed to be making personal meaning by creating mental markers of what constituted success *and* higher-level thinking.

Figure 6.1	Reflective Questioning

Think about a success that you have experienced in your efforts to engage students in higher-level thinking. Describe what you did and the results for students. What factors contributed to this successful outcome?	Now, identify a concern or frustration you have experienced in your attempts to engage your students in thinking. Again, describe what you did and the results. What do you think interfered with success?

I t has often been said that what gets monitored gets done. A key challenge for leaders at all levels is to monitor progress toward goal attainment—and, more important, to establish a collaborative culture in which students and staff are engaged in monitoring progress toward goals. Progress monitoring has taken on greater importance in the era of high-stakes accountability. Teachers are encouraged to systematically monitor student progress toward content standards. School leaders are charged with monitoring programs and progress toward goal attainment. In the scenario you just read, Angela created a climate and used a process that allowed teachers to reflect in a nonthreatening manner about their (and their students') accomplishment of goals related to higher-level thinking. In fact, involvement in the process seemed to help the teachers clarify the goals themselves—and what would constitute success.

Marzano and colleagues (Marzano, Waters, & McNulty, 2005) found monitoring and evaluating to be a key responsibility of effective school leaders. Their meta-analysis of leader effectiveness isolated "the extent to which the leader monitors the effectiveness of school practices in terms of their feedback on student achievement" (p. 55). They associated two discrete behaviors with the monitoring responsibility: (1) "continuously monitoring the effectiveness of the school's curricular, instructional, and assessment practices" and (2) "being continually aware of the impact of the school's practices on student achievement" (p. 56).

Margaret Wheatley (2007) also highlights the importance of feedback to growth and enhanced performance. She distinguishes *feedback* from *measurement*. Measurement, she argues, focuses on numbers, rankings, and ratings as ends in and of themselves. Feedback, which is oftentimes extrapolated from numerical data, is contextualized to the individual and the setting. This expert in organizational change submits that, the focus [of feedback] is on "adaptability and growth," whereas the focus of measurement is on "stability and control" (p. 159). She suggests that leaders ask the following kinds of questions in order to create meaningful measures that are capable of generating useful feedback.

- Who gets to create the measures?
- How will we measure our measures?
- Are we designing measures that are permeable rather than rigid?
- Will these measures create information that increases our capacity to develop, to grow the purpose of this organization?
- What measures will inform us about critical capacities—accountability, learning, teamwork, quality, and innovation (pp. 160–161)?

She advocates for the widespread participation of all members of an organization in designing measures that will produce meaningful feedback, suggesting that individuals are much more apt to attend to data whose importance they have helped to determine.

Feedback produced through ongoing monitoring efforts is a critical component of continuous improvement. Mike Schmoker (2006) writes convincingly of the need for teams of educators to collect and analyze data that measure progress toward goals. Schmoker expresses his belief that "we will not have a guaranteed and viable curriculum until principals or teacher leaders begin to meet with teacher teams by month or quarter to review and discuss evidence of what is actually being taught" (p. 130). Schmoker refers to this as "the courage to monitor."

Doug Reeves (2006) provides a framework for leadership grounded in this proposition. In his Leadership for Learning Framework, he proposes that leaders identify, monitor, and measure what he calls "antecedents for learning" in order to determine their impact on results for students. Through asking questions about the variables (or inputs) to learning, we can become "learning leaders" who are continuously learning from both our mistakes and our successes.

Angela was pleased with the outcome of the Reflective Questioning session and wanted to take the reflection a step further. At the next team meeting, she asked teachers to engage in a visioning process, one she had used numerous times, called Helicopter Visioning (described in Resource B). When the teachers agreed, Angela presented the following prompt:

> *Imagine that you are hovering over our school in a helicopter. From this vantage point, you can see into the school and into classrooms. You notice that most class-rooms have a high percentage of students who are truly engaged in learning and thinking at high cognitive levels. What are you seeing that leads you to this con-clusion? What are the teachers doing? What are the students doing? What are school administrators doing?*

Angela allowed time for each team member to respond, asked them to summarize in pairs, and then facilitated a sharing of the responses. Angela was pleased to note that the group had identified almost every practice from the training. Angela's next question was, "Are we using what we know?" To help team members answer this question, Angela asked them to conduct walkabouts during the coming week as a way to collect data that would focus teacher attention—both as observers and as teachers being observed. By taking the results of the visioning activity and using only those elements that were observable, she created a list of look-fors. Angela suggested that every team member go into the classroom of each of the other five team members for about 5 minutes and record which of the look-fors were present. The observation results were anonymous; that is, no teacher names appeared on the data. Angela tallied the results of the 30 observations and reported them back to the team at their next meeting. She did so without drawing conclusions or making judgments (see Figure 6.2). Rather, she posed a question and presented an opportunity for them to reach their own conclusions. "Look at these results," she told them. "What are we doing well? Talk with a partner and decide which two or three results give us the most cause to celebrate our good work." Many teachers were prone to look for the most frequently observed items. Angela intervened with the following question, "If our students are engaged in cooperative learning one-third of the time, is that cause for celebration?" Teachers agreed that the data were not simple to interpret; their discussions became richer and more analytical. Finally, Angela asked them to think about which single idea would most likely cause increased higher-level thinking and contribute to improved student learning and achievement. Again, this spurred discussion and sharing.

Figure 6.2 Walkabout Summary

School: <u>Westwood Elementary</u>   Dates of observation: <u>Feb. 16–24</u>

Number of classrooms in the team: <u>6</u>   Number of observations completed: <u>30</u>

Look-for	Number of classrooms in which this was observed	Percentage of classrooms in which this was observed
1. Students write to prompts before answering aloud.	3	10%
2. Students talk with a partner or in a small group before answering to the entire class.	4	13%
3. The teacher asks questions that require simple remembering or understanding; no deep thinking.	30	100%
4. The teacher asks questions that require application, analysis, conclusions, or creation of new information.	5	17%
5. Graphic organizers are used.	2	7%
6. Students work in organized cooperative groups.	10	33%
7. Assigned work is clearly related to stated goals and objectives.	20	67%
8. Students ask content-related questions.	0	0%
9. The teacher models effective reading metacognitive strategies.	6	20%
10. Students are actively engaged—for instance, talking (on subject), writing, and interacting with each other or with the teacher.	15	50%
11. The teacher uses follow-up prompts to encourage students to go deeper in their thinking as they respond to questions.	6	20%

Clearly, Angela is taking a leadership role in promoting reflection and self-monitoring among the teachers with whom she works. These simple practices avoid the leader's deciding what's important to assess and give teachers responsibility to assess practice. For the next step in this process, Angela had in mind moving teachers to engage in inquiry-based learning, during which they would formulate a hypothesis, plan data-collection strategies, and implement to determine the extent to which the instructional strategies affect student learning.

Angela was intentional in helping teachers collect and analyze data. Sometimes, schools collect data but fail to use or make meaning of them. The story that follows is an example of a schoolwide effort to improve student attendance (and the related graduation rate) by identifying the cause of the school's high level of absenteeism, come up with an effective intervention, and monitor the effectiveness of their plan using multiple sources of data.

LaTonda Williams was a principal new to Cunningham School (Grades 6–12). The school was experiencing a significantly low attendance rate and a correspondingly high dropout rate. She had been brought to the school in part because of her success in curbing the dropout rate at her prior school. There, she and the instructional staff had decided to focus their efforts on providing more engaging, relevant, and rigorous instruction. With hard work and lots of peer monitoring, their efforts had paid off; more students were successful and fewer dropped out of school.

Her initial thought was to duplicate the process in the new school; however, she didn't want to make too many assumptions. She considered her options and decided to begin her work by engaging the faculty in dialogue about their perceptions of the cause of student absenteeism. She chose to use a process called Five Whys (described in Resource B). LaTonda asked her faculty to gather in groups of three, with two group members serving as interviewers and one serving as respondent. She described the process and asked them to begin with one of the interviewers posing this question: Why do so many of our students miss so much school? After listening carefully, the interviewers were to attempt to get behind the reasons by asking why as many as times as necessary; she encouraged them to ask at least four additional times. She listened in as one respondent answered, "They don't want to be here." The interviewers posed another question: "Why do you think they don't want to be at school?" The response: "Their reasons for not coming must be stronger than any reason we've given them to attend." Again came another why (this time, phrased as a "what" question): "What do you think are some of their reasons for staying away?" The response: "I guess they're not feeling comfortable here; they must not believe this is a place that meets their needs." And so they continued. The faculty was engaged in the process, and this led to an important discovery: They really didn't have the answer.

> *If you don't ask the right questions, you don't get the right answers. A question asked in the right way often points to its own answer. Asking questions is the ABC of diagnosis. Only the inquiring mind solves problems.*
>
> —Edward Hodnett (in Cox, 2008, p. 74)

Someone asked aloud, "Why don't we ask the kids? They would probably know." Several faculty members volunteered to put together a student focus group (see the Focus Group process described in Resource B) to provide a student perspective of the attendance problem. In addition, they identified several recent dropouts who agreed to one-on-one interviews. (See Interview or Conference process in Resource B.)

LaTonda and others were surprised by the students' answers to the first question (What can we do to make this school one where all students are willing to attend every day—and stay through graduation?). Students responded that they didn't feel safe; this was confirmed by recent dropouts, who specifically identified safety issues on the buses. It seems a tradition had been started years earlier to taunt and menace students during the bus rides. For many students, it wasn't worth it to face this every day.

One of the teachers probed further, "Why didn't you tell us about this?" One student stated, "I always fill out those surveys that you give us. I told you about it every year." Other kids nodded in agreement. "Some of us had to ride buses for more than an hour every day. When I got old enough to skip school, I did."

LaTonda decided to investigate the results of the school-culture surveys. She discovered that during the previous five annual administrations, between 32% and 36% of the middle school students had indicated that they did not feel safe on the bus. Furthermore, between 25% and 29% had indicated that they did not feel safe on school grounds before and after school. There it was, in black and white. Yet, nothing had been done. For the first time, LaTonda truly understood what Fullan (2004) meant when he said, "Information is on paper and in computers. Knowledge is in people. Data without relationships merely increase the information glut" (p. 115). LaTonda wondered what other knowledge might be hidden in the data.

This is a story in which the answer to an important question was almost missed because of common assumptions about the root of the problem. How many of us, in LaTonda's position, would have begun with the assumption that the school's poor attendance problem was rooted in instructional quality? Fortunately, because of LaTonda's leadership in facilitating quality questioning, the school staff discovered a problem that had remained hidden for years—and they held themselves accountable for addressing it.

After discussing the students' insights during a faculty meeting, staff agreed to work collectively on the safety issues. With input from the bus drivers, they designed a training program. They recruited volunteers from the community to ride buses until the problems were solved. Most important, they designed ways to monitor and assess progress that helped address the problem. They engaged family members in monitoring attendance by instituting a daily homework log signed by the last teacher of the day. They continued focus groups on a monthly basis to better understand what was helping and what was not helping. They continued the annual assessment, engaging parents and students to help make meaning of the data. They posted weekly attendance rates outside of each homeroom; the students helped design creative ways to graph and display the data. They disaggregated the data by bus routes and by other demographic factors, following up with focus groups when they needed more in-depth information. In short, through focusing on solving the problem, and by collecting quantitative and qualitative data to help better understand as well as monitor results, the school saw positive results and continued to make improvements in the interventions.

This scenario clearly illustrates both the pitfalls and promises of monitoring. While this school had taken great pride in annual monitoring of school climate, they had engaged in limited analysis of the data that were collected. In the process of addressing a critical problem, school leaders uncovered not only the root causes of the problem but also their failure to drill down into the data they had collected through the climate survey. As a result, they created multiple and complementary monitoring tools to accompany implementation of the plan developed to address the root causes of absenteeism. Along the way, they learned that data are only as good as the questions and dialogue they generate.

While there is more emphasis today being placed on data, these data tend to be of a singular nature and the accompanying dialogue is often superficial. Any possibility for thoughtful conversation that would tease out underlying complexities is sabotaged by the desperate hunt for a solution, the quick fix. Hurried interactions of the sort that often characterize faculty room encounters and faculty meetings tend to draw on the sameness of teaching, reaffirming and reiterating familiar educational practices. Hurried solutions shield us from differences and therefore from challenges to our old ways of thinking while it "protects" us from growth.

—David Perkins (2003, p. 35)

EXAMPLES OF QUALITY QUESTIONS FOR MONITORING PROGRESS

1. What kind of evidence would help us know that we are making progress toward our goal?

2. What student behaviors are you looking for as you implement this new behavior plan?

3. What should we expect to see when we conduct the walkabouts to let us know that this program is being implemented?

4. What do these data tell us about student use of effective questioning strategies?

5. Speculate on the antecedents of excellence. What factors may be contributing to this success?

6. If we believe that a flexible schedule could assist in efforts to differentiate instruction, what type of evidence could we collect to test this hypothesis?

7. In what ways can we self-monitor our use of this new strategy?

7

Promoting Adult Learning and Growth in Schools

How Can Leaders Nurture Communities of Quality Questioners?

Genuine inquiry-centered leadership requires following where the inquiry leads, rather than manipulating the process toward answers the leader has already fixated on. Soon enough, false openness will be discovered, breaking the relationship of trust that inquiry-centered leadership cultivates.

—David Perkins, *King Arthur's Round Table*

FOCUS QUESTIONS

1. In what ways does adult use of quality questioning impact and support classroom practice?

2. What can leaders do to assist all members of a learning community in improving their use of quality questioning skills?

3. What is your Quality Questioning Quotient?

Carla Collins, principal of Plains Elementary School, committed to the principles and practice of quality questioning several years ago. Initially, Carla's focus was on supporting teachers' use of quality questioning with their students. She attended a three-day training-of-trainers session with a team of her teachers and assisted them in implementing a job-embedded professional-development experience for the entire faculty and staff. The intent was to focus professional learning on quality questioning over a two-year period. Carla purchased copies of the book Quality Questioning *for all members of the faculty, provided time for professional-learning-community sessions on the topic of quality questioning, scheduled opportunities for teachers to observe one another, and provided feedback to teachers regarding their questioning practices after each observation and walkthrough. Yet at the end of the first year of implementation, she sensed that something was missing. She had envisioned a school in which the dynamic of inquiry permeated all classrooms. Her sense was that there were still clusters of teacher resistance. She wondered what else she could do.*

She decided to invite seemingly uncommitted teachers to participate in a dialogue focused on their reservations and questions. She began the session by calling attention to the norms for conversation, emphasizing that she wanted everyone to feel free to express themselves openly and honestly. Carla then stated, "We are in the midst of a professional-development initiative that is focused on quality questioning for all of our students. Some of our faculty are very enthusiastic about the potential of these strategies for their students. Other teachers seem less committed. I am genuinely interested in the questions and concerns you may have about this focus and hope you will share your perceptions with me." Carla then stopped talking and waited. Silence reigned. During the 30 seconds or so of quiet, Carla reflected on her question. She had carefully framed the prompt—and had intentionally ruled out asking, "Why aren't you using these strategies?" She did not want to put the teachers on the defensive. As she waited still longer, she pondered a follow-up question. Perhaps she could ask, "What are the barriers to more widespread acceptance of this initiative?" Then she thought, "No. I've asked my question. I need to wait. I don't need to stack questions." So she continued to wait, scanning the group and making eye contact with each of the eight teachers who had assembled.

Finally, one of the more vocal members of the faculty spoke, "Do you really want to know what we think?" Carla nodded and waited. The teacher then continued, "No one asked us if we needed this professional development. It was thrust upon us." Carla was a bit taken aback but remained quiet. Another teacher spoke, "I agree with that. You want us to engage all of our students in speaking during class discussion, but you didn't ask all of us what we thought about this. It's like you talked to your leadership team and got their approval. Then it was full speed ahead." Again, there was silence. A third teacher spoke, saying, "I'd like to piggyback on that. You know that was kind of like our relying on a few students in our class for answers to all of our questions. You've told us that this is not what you expect; that you expect us to find ways to get everyone involved. It almost seems like you haven't practiced what you've preached." Now Carla was asking herself, "Why didn't I invite some of the supporters of the initiative to this session?" Her thoughts were interrupted by another teacher voice, "I agree with that, and I also think those teachers who you think are so good at this are a little hypocritical themselves. The other day, I asked Robert, one of my teammates, how he knew this stuff was working in his class. He shrugged his shoulders and replied, 'I just know, and anyway, the research says it does.' That didn't sound like a questioning approach to me." The dialogue continued, and Carla listened intently—making eye contact with each speaker and nodding to show understanding—but she refrained from speaking. At the end of the 30-minute scheduled time, she smiled at these eight teachers and thanked them for their insights. She promised to reflect on what they had said and to think about the implications.

C arla's story is a synthesis of stories we've heard from principals of schools that have used our book *Quality Questioning* as the centerpiece for a major professional-development initiative. These school leaders have experienced a big aha—that quality questioning will not long thrive in classrooms situated in schools where leaders do not embrace an inquiry-centered approach. Their reflection led them to infer that if inquiry is to permeate the classrooms and teacher work areas of their schools then school leaders themselves must model all aspects of this practice. We have strong anecdotal evidence to suggest that when leaders not only talk the talk but also walk the walk of quality questioning, student learning benefits. Let's continue with our scenario.

Following considerable reflection on teacher comments that had emerged from the dialogue session, Carla decided to be more mindful of her own use of quality questioning and more overt and explicit about her vision of creating a school of quality questioners. She determined that a good place to begin would be to have the faculty share their perceptions about the extent to which school leaders employed principles of inquiry. Carla prepared a set of items related to leader use of inquiry when adopting new initiatives and included the items in a rating form (see Figure 7.1). Her intent was to have each teacher anonymously rate the extent to which he or she believed that school leaders practiced each of these principles. Carla then planned to invite teachers to participate in a dialogue to assist her and other members of the leadership team in making meaning of the responses.

Carla and the leadership team summarized teacher responses to the survey and prepared wall charts to display the results for an upcoming faculty session. The mean responses to Items 3 and 8 were the highest. From this, Carla inferred that there was at least a foundation on which to build trust across the faculty. Mean responses to the other items hovered between two and three. The planned focus for the faculty session was to make meaning from the survey responses and determine next steps.

When teachers arrived for the session, they were randomly seated in table groups of five. Carla opened the session by stating the purpose: to reflect together on the extent to which faculty were using inquiry in schoolwide interactions and to suggest what it might take to become a more inquiry-centered community. She asked the table groups to organize for their work by naming a facilitator, recorder, and timekeeper. She told them they would have 25 minutes for table dialogue, after which each group would provide a 2-minute summary of its conversation to the whole group and a written copy of main ideas to the leadership team.

Each table group was then assigned one of the items from the survey and asked to first talk about the meaning of the ratings for their assigned item. The following focus questions were provided to guide the discussion:

Figure 7.1	Rating: To What Extent Do We Engage in Inquiry-Centered Practices in Our School?

Directions: Circle the number, 1–5, that best reflects your opinion of current practice in our school.

When considering a new initiative, school leaders adopt an approach of

1. Telling, persuading, or "selling" staff	1 2 3 4 5	Posing questions and seeking input from those involved
2. Looking "outside" for a silver bullet	1 2 3 4 5	Generating and testing solutions from within
3. Adopting a posture of "Do as I say, not as I do"	1 2 3 4 5	Modeling the new way of working; that is, "walking the talk"
4. Seeking unanimity in opinion; discouraging disagreements	1 2 3 4 5	Respecting and encouraging different points of view
5. Trying something and hoping it makes a difference	1 2 3 4 5	Planning for and actively monitoring the use of new initiatives

When considering a new initiative, members of the school community adopt an approach of

6. Passivity and compliance	1 2 3 4 5	Active commitment
7. Competitiveness	1 2 3 4 5	Cooperation
8. Rarely expressing opinions openly	1 2 3 4 5	Feeling free to express different points of view
9. Pushing their own agendas	1 2 3 4 5	Suspending judgment while listening to other points of view
10. "This too shall pass"	1 2 3 4 5	Taking ownership to make it successful
11. Resisting change	1 2 3 4 5	Openness to new ideas to benefit students

- *On what evidence might teachers have based their responses?*
- *What concrete examples can the group offer?*
- *If indeed this is a true picture of how we operate, what are the implications for the students and adults in the school?*

The table groups were instructed to think about what each of them could do to move the school to a more inquiry-centered operation.

As Carla walked around to determine if all groups understood the assignment and were on task, she was pleased to see that almost everyone in the room was actively engaged in talking and that everyone seemed to be taking the task seriously. Group reports demonstrated deep thinking about issues associated with the assigned items; a number of the recommendations represented true out-of-the-box thinking.

After the session, Carla carefully reviewed the team reports. A number of suggestions addressed ways in which she could more consistently display inquiry-centered leadership. She was surprised, however, that the majority of recommendations focused on what it might mean to become an inquiry-centered professional learning community. Five of the eight groups specifically suggested additional community sessions during which they could explore practices associated with schoolwide inquiry.

Carla invited the facilitators from each of the eight groups to meet with her to plan a follow-up session. This group decided to use the Interview Design process (described in Resource B) to prompt deeper thinking about the topic. They looked to the literature on inquiry and learning communities for powerful quotes that might serve as lead-ins to the questions. They then crafted four prompts (including questions) for the Interview Design process.

Interview Design Questions

Plains Elementary School

Question 1. "In the advanced-inquiry schools we studied, faculty discussions often probed deeply into patterns of student outcomes. They posed questions such as, Why do Black and Hispanic students differ in what they accomplish in upper-elementary grades? Why do tenth-grade Latino boys consistently fall off in mathematics? Why are students' writing skills in one third-grade class more advanced than in the others? Teachers in these schools posed such questions without finger pointing or blame but in an effort to understand connections between classroom practices and what their students were able to do." (McLaughlin & Talbert, 2001, p. 34)

Teachers in these schools asked questions that were authentic—for which they had no single answer. What kinds of questions do you have about improving teaching and learning in our school?

Question 2. "At the very least, one must imagine schools in which teachers are in frequent conversation with each other about their work, have easy and necessary access to each other's classrooms, take it for granted that they should

---

comment on each other's work, and have the time to develop common standards for student work." (Meier, in Darling-Hammond & Sykes, 1999, p. 233)

2.A. What would have to happen for our school to become such a school?
2.B. What would be the benefits to students and to teachers in our school if we developed such a culture of inquiry and became a true community of learners?

Question 3. *Lee and Smith (2001) found from their research that students perform better in schools where teachers take collective responsibility for the success of all students. Indeed, in schools with teacher community, they found that the effect of socioeconomic status was lessened; inequalities mattered less. Lee and Smith write, "Collective responsibility for learning . . . included: teachers' internalizing responsibility for the learning of their students, rather than attributing learning difficulties to weak students or deficient home conditions; a belief that teachers can teach all students; a willingness to alter teaching methods in response to students' difficulties and successes; and feelings of efficacy in teaching." (p. 87)*

3.A. What norms, attitudes, values, and behaviors would we need to adopt as a faculty if we truly assumed collective responsibility for student learning?
3.B. Which of these do you think would be most difficult to develop?

Question 4. *The "lone wolf scenario" is still prominent in most schools, "in which teachers labor on their own to decide what instruction works, what standard of student work is good enough, and what additional knowledge, skill, or insights would best serve them and their students. . . . The exception to this scenario arises in the context of ambitious programs of innovation that supply favorable conditions for professional development: collaborative work among peers, external assistance, a new infusion of materials and technologies, sustained inquiry into problems of student learning in specific subjects, and the close evaluation of experiments in curriculum and instruction." (Little, 1999, p. 234)*

What would it take for our school to become a place in which teachers work together and ask and answer important questions about teaching and learning?

As Carla welcomed faculty to this community session, she noted more smiles and energy than usual for a 3:00 meeting. Again, faculty engagement was high, and responses appeared honest and well reasoned. She had collected a lot of faculty input over the past month. Now, she thought she would be very challenged to use faculty thinking to make important changes in her own approach and, in collaboration with appropriate individuals, in structures and resources to support increased faculty inquiry.

Inquiry-centered leadership means that inquiry is the center of gravity, not that nothing else ever happens.

—David Perkins (2003, p. 100)

The Plains Elementary School scenario illustrates how a leader can use quality questioning practices to initiate transformation of a school culture. Such a transformation is a process that occurs over time with stops and starts, successes and failures. It never occurs without intentionality on the part of a committed core group of leaders who envision an inquiry-oriented environment for adults and students. If this transformation is to occur, members of the community must adopt new norms and attitudes about doing the business of schooling—and they must develop knowledge and skills associated with quality questioning. This book was written as a manual of practice for leaders who have this vision and commitment.

To enhance your practice and to review the contents of this book, we invite you to make use of The Quality Questioning Quotient (QQQ): A Self-Assessment (Resource C). This instrument is designed to promote individual reflection and serve as a springboard to individual and collective learning about the practices associated with the Leading Through Quality Questioning (LQQ) Framework. We also invite you to adapt this instrument for use with members of your school as you continue the journey to create capacity, commitment, and community throughout your learning organization.

Resource A

Examples of Closed and Open-Ended Questions

Approach 1 (Closed Questions)

Leader: Do your students know the procedures for cooperative work?

Teacher: Well, most of them probably do.

Leader: Don't you think it would help if all students knew specific procedures for cooperative work?

Teacher: Yes, I guess so.

Leader: Have you ever asked students to assess themselves on their use of the procedures for cooperative learning?

Teacher: Not really; I pretty much have a feel for who's acting appropriately and who's not.

Approach 2 (Open-Ended Questions)

Leader: What are the rules and procedures that you believe are most helpful to students as they work in cooperative groups?

Teacher: It's certainly important that they establish leadership roles: recorder, materials manager, timekeeper, and facilitator. And, I think it's important that these roles be rotated so that every student has an opportunity to assume each leadership role. Also, I think it's important that everyone contribute; it's not right to depend on one or two students to do all the thinking for the group.

Leader: How have you helped students learn procedures for working together in groups?

Teacher: (Pauses to consider the question.) Well, to tell you the truth, I haven't spent a lot of time specifically teaching these procedures. Of course, at the beginning of the year, we reviewed the four leadership roles—and defined each. And, I continually remind them how important it is that each student contributes. But generally, we follow the same rules in cooperative learning that we do in whole-group instruction: don't interrupt, listen to others, have all of your materials available, and don't talk out unless you are recognized by the teacher. Oh, well, that one doesn't work for cooperative groups. I guess we really need to have a set of rules and procedures that we follow when we work like this. In fact, I think the kids themselves could help formulate a list. They've done this enough to know what works and what doesn't.

Leader: What might be the benefits if students did have clear expectations for how to work in groups?

Teacher: Well, we all work better if we have a vision of how it can be. I think having clear expectations—and having them posted on each cluster of desks while students work together—would help them remember. And beyond that, they don't all know how to work together. Some do; but others haven't really engaged in teamwork before. Or they may feel inadequate and not feel that they can contribute. Yes, I definitely think that it will help if we have posted rules and procedures for working cooperatively. And, I'm going to let the kids help me develop them.

Leader: How might students monitor their use of effective procedures for cooperative work?

Teacher: Oh, that would really seal the deal. If they can help me create the procedures, they are certainly in the best position to assess their group's functioning. You know, I think I remember hearing something about that at the inservice session we had last semester.

Now, read through these two approaches again. This time, we have added a column to represent what each person might have been thinking as he or she spoke. Can you see that questions have a powerful effect on attitude—for example, defensiveness versus openness; trying to guess the "right" answer versus articulating one's own thoughts; boredom versus excitement and enthusiasm?

Table A.1	Approach 1

	Actual Comment	**What They Might Be Thinking**
Leader:	*Do your students know the procedures for cooperative work?*	This teacher was using cooperative learning when I observed. That's really good; I've been trying to encourage teachers to use these strategies. Unfortunately, not all of the kids seem to know how to act in cooperative groups. Establishing procedures is a key to success in using cooperative learning. I wonder if she has taught them to the students.
Teacher:	*Well, most of them probably do.*	What's so hard about working in groups? There are some kids who don't know how to behave in school; they act inappropriately and get the others off task. That's par for the course.
Leader:	*Don't you think it would help if all students knew specific procedures for cooperative work?*	Remember, we had a great inservice session last semester that really stressed this.
Teacher:	*Yes, I guess so.*	Whew, there's no other way to answer that question, is there? Seems like she's leading the witness. I guess she's not happy with something that happened today. Wish she would stop asking—and just tell me in plain English!
Leader:	*Have you ever asked students to assess themselves on their use of the procedures for cooperative learning?*	This was another strategy we learned at the inservice. I thought this was really great!
Teacher:	*Not really; I pretty much have a feel for who's acting appropriately and who's not.*	What in the world is she talking about?

Table A.2   Approach 2

Can you see how defensiveness is replaced by openness, new ideas, and commitment to try something new?

	Actual Comment	What They Might Be Thinking
Leader:	*What are the rules and procedures that you believe are most helpful to students as they work in cooperative groups?*	This teacher was using cooperative learning when I observed. That's really good; I've been trying to encourage teachers to use these strategies. Unfortunately, not all the kids seem to know how to act in cooperative groups. Establishing procedures is a key to success in using cooperative learning. I wonder if she has taught them to the students. And, I'm wondering what she knows about the importance of teaching rules and procedures that help students work successfully in groups. I wonder what she believes are the most important ones.
Teacher:	*It's certainly important that they establish leadership roles: recorder, materials manager, timekeeper, and facilitator. And, I think it's important that these roles be rotated so that every student has an opportunity to assume each leadership role. Also, I think it's important that everyone contribute; it's not right to depend on one or two students to do all the thinking for the group.*	This is interesting to think about. I'm not sure I've ever articulated these to myself. I wonder why she is asking.
Leader:	*How have you helped students learn procedures for working together in groups?*	I'm wondering if these have been communicated to students clearly. And, I wonder if she could add to the examples of important procedures.
Teacher:	*Well, to tell you the truth, I haven't spent a lot of time specifically teaching these procedures. Of course, at the beginning of the year, we reviewed the four leadership*	That's an interesting question. Let me think about it.

	Actual Comment	**What They Might Be Thinking**
	roles—and defined each. And I continually remind them how important it is that each student contributes. But generally, we follow the same rules in cooperative learning that we do in whole-group instruction: don't interrupt, listen to others, have all of your materials available, and don't talk out unless you are recognized by the teacher. Oh, well, that one doesn't work for cooperative groups. I guess we really need to have a set of rules and procedures that we follow when we work like this. In fact, I think the kids themselves could help formulate a list. They've done this enough to know what works and what doesn't.	I wonder what other teachers have done. Do they have a set of special rules and procedures that help students work cooperatively?
Leader:	*What might be the benefits if students did have clear expectations for how to work in groups?*	Oh, she's getting it! Now, I'd like for her to say aloud the reasons so that she remembers how important it is to do this.
Teacher:	*Well, we all work better if we have a vision of how it can be. I think having clear expectations—and having them posted on each cluster of desks while students work together—would help them remember. And beyond that, they don't all know how to work together. Some do; but others haven't really engaged in teamwork before. Or they may feel inadequate and not feel that they can contribute. Yes, I definitely think that it will help if we have posted rules and procedures for working cooperatively. And I'm going to let the kids help me develop them.*	This makes so much sense. How could I have missed that? This is really going to help, I think.
Leader:	*How might students monitor their use of effective procedures for cooperative work?*	I wonder if I could push just a little bit more. This was something that was mentioned in the inservice session and I think it might be worth bringing up now.
Teacher:	*Oh, that would really seal the deal. If they can help me create the procedures, they are certainly in the best position to assess their own group's functioning. You know, I think I remember hearing something about that at the inservice session we had last semester.*	Yes, I can!

Resource B

Structured Group Processes That Engage Members of the School Community in Thinking and Dialogue

1. Conversations

Purpose

Establishes a setting in which individuals think about and discuss important ideas, contributing from their own perspective and building on one another's ideas to create a new understanding; scaffolds true dialogue; creates a "whole" of collective thinking about a given topic as people share insights through a structured process designed to foster understanding and spark creativity.

Preparation

Prepare an essential question (one that gets at the heart of the matter being addressed) for each table at which participants will hold a conversation. Make a copy of the question, and place it on the table. Provide a variety of markers and crayons as well as one or two sheets of easel paper to form a tablecloth on which participants can record their conversation ideas.

Facilitation

Once four to six participants are seated at each table, introduce the process. Explain that an essential question will guide each table's conversation. Each table should begin by having someone read the question aloud as others in the small group listen and focus on the important issues contained within the question. Group members are to record their responses with markers on the tablecloth. Encourage them to be creative and to use words, pictures, color, and other visuals. Group members should also verbalize their responses. Instruct them to speak openly and honestly, to listen to others carefully to fully understand their points of view, to watch for connections between ideas, and to honor silence (i.e., use wait time as appropriate).

When time is called, each group will identify one person to remain as table host. The others will disperse to different tables so that participants will be with different people for each round of conversation. During the second round, most people (with the exception of the table host) will be talking about a new question. Instruct participants to listen to the question, review the ideas on the tablecloth, discuss them, and add their own ideas.

The role of the table host is to welcome people to the table, answer any questions about the prior conversations held at the table, and remind people to write down ideas and questions—not to merely talk to one another—and to make connections between ideas.

Adapted from Brown & Isaacs, 2005

2. Data on Display

Purpose

Helps establish a risk-free environment in which group members reflect individually on core issues, see a visual display of the thinking of the whole group, and move from thinking about their own responses to thinking about implications of the group's responses; prompts hypothesis formulation and the examination of their own and others' assumptions.

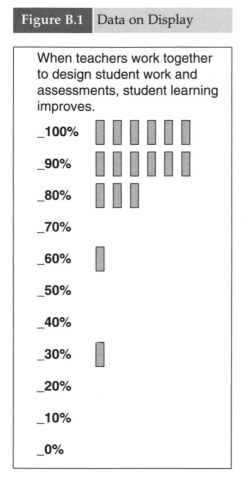

Figure B.1 Data on Display

When teachers work together to design student work and assessments, student learning improves.

_100%
_90%
_80%
_70%
_60%
_50%
_40%
_30%
_20%
_10%
_0%

Preparation

Select a topic, and prepare four to six statements about which participants can agree or disagree. For best results, the statements will create cognitive dissonance among participants (i.e., a belief with which they strongly agree followed by a statement of action that does not align with the belief). Prepare a handout for each participant with each statement followed by a scale from 100 to 0. Write each question or statement at the top of a sheet of easel paper; down the left edge of the chart, include a scale ranging from 100 to 0, marked off in 10-point increments. Leave enough space between the numbers for participants to place sticky notes (see Figure B.1). For each participant, provide one blank sticky note for each question (preferably 0.5″ × 1.75″). Hang the charts around the room. Seat participants at tables in small groups.

Facilitation

Ask participants to respond individually to each of the statements by first selecting the extent to which they agree with the statement (from 0% to 100%) then by using sticky notes to post their responses on the charts, contributing to a bar graph for each statement. Allow time for individuals to view the charts and come to conclusions about what the data mean. Allow additional time for participants to discuss the data in small groups. Finally, facilitate a large-group discussion to identify conclusions and implications.

3. Final Word

Purpose

Encourages listening to and learning from different points of view about a common reading; helps participants to think through, in depth, their own understanding of a specific passage of text; and facilitates true comprehension and meaning making.

Preparation

Identify a common reading related to the topic under consideration. Ask participants to read it before coming to the session and to identify three ideas about which they would like to talk or hear discussion. Seat participants in small groups of four or five. Provide copies of the directions for the process.

Facilitation

Ask each group to identify (1) a facilitator, who will monitor the group's use of the Final Word protocol; (2) a timekeeper, who will alert participants to the time; and (3) a volunteer, to go first in the discussion of an idea from the reading. Throughout this process, when one person is speaking, others in the group are quiet; they are listening or taking notes.

The first volunteer in the group selects one of his or her ideas, directs the attention of the group to the place in the reading where it appears, and talks about this idea for up to three minutes. When the first person finishes talking (or when time is called), each of the other group members will respond, in turn, for up to one minute each—staying on the topic introduced by the first speaker. When all members of the group have responded, the original speaker has up to one minute to give "the final word" on the topic.

A second person then selects one of his or her ideas and follows the same process. If time allows, every person introduces an idea from the reading for discussion by the group.

4. Fishbone

Purpose

Facilitates group brainstorming of specific ways to achieve a common goal.

Preparation

Decide on the quality question, or subject, that participants will consider. Draw a sample fishbone for the group (see Figure B.2). Seat participants at tables in small groups (4–6).

Facilitation

Ask each small group to brainstorm strategies for accomplishing the goal that is specified in the point of the fishbone. After they have written the big ideas on the ribs of the fish, they can write more specific ideas branching out from each (as suggested by dashed lines). As small groups share their ideas with the large group, look for commonalities—and unique ideas.

Figure B.2	Fishbone

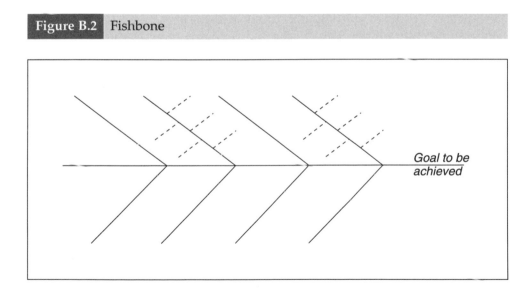

Goal to be achieved

5. Fishbowl

Purpose

Engages participants in true dialogue with one another; helps a group learn the skills of dialogue and be intentional in practicing them; and encourages active listening and questioning.

Preparation

Prepare a pivotal question around which a group could have varied opinions and engage in dialogue. Arrange chairs into two concentric circles, with 6 to 10 chairs in the inside circle and the remaining chairs in the outside circle.

Facilitation

Begin by sharing group norms to guide the experience and reviewing the skills and behaviors of dialogue (e.g., have an open mind; listen with respect to others' responses, seeking to fully understand; use Wait Time 2, allowing at least 3–5 seconds of silence after each speaker; and monitor your participation, contributing ideas and allowing others to do the same).

Select a group of participants to sit in the inner circle (or fishbowl), leaving one chair empty. Direct other participants to sit in the outer circle. Explain that the inside circle is to model dialogue—clarifying assumptions, speaking without defensiveness, and working to understand others' points of view. The outside circle is to (1) listen to the exchange of ideas, (2) enter the inner circle to pose questions or make statements (which pushes the thinking of the fishbowl members), and (3) monitor the use of norms and dialogic skills used by the members of the fishbowl. (Whenever one of those in the outside circle wishes to pose a question or make a statement, he or she should move to the empty chair in the fishbowl to do so and then return to the outer circle.)

Pose the pivotal question. Allow time for the group to respond. Prompt for clarification, as necessary; monitor the use of norms.

Tip

For a rich discussion, give the question or questions to small groups for discussion prior to the fishbowl. Include a member from each small group in the inner circle; this will accomplish representation of the full group. Alternatively, allow time for individuals to respond in writing to a prompt prior to entering the fishbowl discussion.

6. Five Whys

Purpose

Provides practice in asking probing questions; helps to uncover the underlying problem or root cause of an issue; and goes beyond the easy answer to help people explore their own assumptions.

Preparation

Develop a problem statement.

Facilitation

If the group is large, ask participants to gather in small groups of two, three, or four people. In each group, members should designate one person to respond; the others are to be interviewers, listening and posing questions. Explain the process: One of the interviewers will ask why the problem occurs; the respondent will identify a potential cause. Then, an interviewer will ask why that cause occurs, and so on. Typically, it takes 5 times to get to a (sometimes unexpected) root cause; but 5 is not a magic number. Each group may ask fewer or more than 5 *whys*.

Tip

Explain that interviewers can use respondents' answers to phrase their follow-up questions. For example, interviewers shouldn't merely say "Why?" each time. For example, if someone asks, "Why do so many students fail algebra?" the response might be, "Many of them never mastered the basics of math." A good follow-up question might be, "Why do we have so many students who don't have a mastery of basic math?" (instead of a simple "Why?").

7. Focus Group

Purpose

Serves to gather information and perceptions from a small but representative group (8 to 10); encourages the open and honest expression of different points of view; and goes deep into a topic, bringing to the surface issues that may be difficult to express in the larger group.

Preparation

Create 5 to 10 open-ended questions around the topic of interest. For each question, create follow-up prompts that will help participants go deeper after initial responses. Select participants by inviting a representative group from the population of interest (e.g., teachers, parents, or students). Arrange chairs in a circle so that everyone can see others in the group. Write ground rules for the group. For example: One person speaks at a time, allow three to five seconds between speakers for all to digest what has been said, listen without judgment, monitor the amount of time you talk, contribute but allow others to do the same, add to others' comments, refrain from using the names of students or teachers, agree to keep what is said in confidence.

Facilitation

Welcome the group. Explain the purpose for the focus group and its ground rules. Pose an initial question and, in silence, allow time for people to think about it and to make notes to themselves. Open the floor for dialogue. Use probes and follow-up questions as appropriate. Encourage elaboration by using silence and verbal prompts.

8. Force Field Analysis

Purpose

Analyzing the pros and cons of (or forces for and against) a decision, learning enough to be able to strengthen those forces that support a decision and reduce the oppositional forces.

Preparation

On an easel pad, create a sample force field (see Figure B.3) with the vision of an initiative in the center. Use this sample to describe the activity. Participants will replicate a version for their small-group work.

Facilitation

Ask participants to brainstorm forces within the school and/or community that work to oppose the change—and to list them on the right side of a worksheet. Then ask participants to list the forces that work to strengthen the change on the left side of the worksheet. The group should then analyze the forces listed on both sides and decide whether the proposed change or initiative is viable. If a decision has already been made to implement the initiative, Force Field Analysis can help the group determine how to improve its probability of success.

Tip

If you want to create a quantitative look at the forces, ask participants to assign a score to each force, from one (weak) to five (strong). This can help the group set priorities as it moves forward with its plans.

Figure B.3   Force Field Analysis

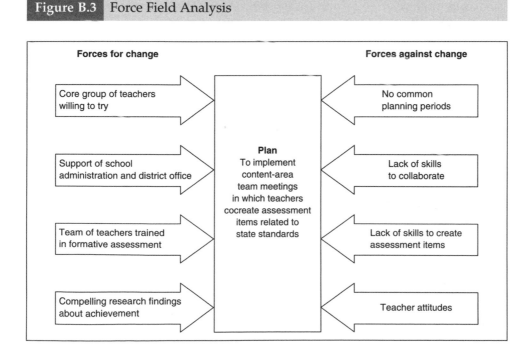

9. Four-Corner Synectics

Purpose

Engages participants in metaphorical thinking about the issue under consideration; facilitates creative thinking that stimulates group discussion and problem solving.

Preparation

Prepare a prompt around the issue under consideration. For example, the prompt might be, "Describe your vision of effective professional development." Select four words or images that participants can use to create metaphors (see examples below). Put each word or image on a separate sheet of flip chart paper, and post one in each corner of the room, along with a flip chart marker.

Facilitation

Present the prompt and ask participants to write their responses. After adequate time for individual thinking, ask, "As you think about this issue, is it more like _____ or _____ or _____ or _____ [name the four metaphors]?" For example: *Is effective professional development more like scuba diving, mountain climbing, deep-sea fishing, or white water rafting?* Ask each participant to select the one metaphor that best matches his or her thinking on the topic.

Direct participants to move to the corner of the room that displays their chosen metaphor. Once participants are grouped with others who selected the same metaphor, tell them to list the reasons for their choice on the flip chart paper (that is, to tell how their selected metaphor is like *the topic under consideration*). Ask each of the four groups to share its thinking with the others. Move to a large-group discussion on the topic.

Tip

Here are some other possible metaphors: earth, wind, fire, water; playing basketball, conducting an orchestra, directing a movie, working a family farm; and a pick-up truck, a Cadillac, a Prius, an SUV.

Variations

Simple synectics involves choosing two contrasting items and asking participants to respond individually, in writing, and then to share their ideas in small groups. For example, you might ask one of these questions: *Are parent conferences more like spaghetti or ice cream? Is grading student work more like summer or winter? Is school improvement more like a roller coaster or an 18-wheel truck?*

10. Helicopter Visioning

Purpose

Prompts individual reflection that, when shared with others, can result in a common vocabulary and shared expectations and vision.

Preparation

Select an issue that needs attention at your school. Prompt participants to imagine themselves in a helicopter hovering above a school or classroom, able to see what is going on in that setting. Write the prompt on a handout for each participant or display it on a slide or easel so that all can see it. For example: *Imagine you are hovering in a helicopter over your classroom six months from now—after you have successfully implemented hands-on activities to help students better learn and understand science. What would you see in that classroom; that is, what are you, as the teacher, doing? What are your students doing? What does the classroom feel like? What are the sounds and sights?*

Facilitation

Allow about three minutes for participants to think and write individually in response to the prompt. Then ask those present to form small groups and to identify a facilitator and recorder. Within each small group, individuals should share their responses and brainstorm ideas in a tell-around fashion, with each person contributing one idea in turn. Ask the groups to record each unique idea on a sticky note. Bring the sticky notes from all groups together and post them on a wall. Ask participants to cluster them into like categories and to name the categories. Assign at least one cluster to each group for naming.

Tip

If too many clusters or ideas are generated, you can use a voting system by giving participants three to five colored dots each and asking them to post their dots next to the ideas or clusters they deem most important. List the top vote-getting ideas and ask the group to add any others that seem essential.

11. Ink Think (Nonverbal Mind Mapping)

Purpose

Organizes information in a visual, nonlinear way; stimulates thinking; helps to develop new patterns of thought; and gets people to go deeper into a subject.

Preparation

Create one to four key questions that will help participants consider the vision, barriers, or benefits of a given concept. Prepare participant worksheets that include all four questions for individual reflection. Post wall charts (one for each question) around the room so that participants can record their thoughts. For each question, put a word, phrase, or symbol in the center of the chart to represent what you want the group to think about. If you have more than one group, provide each group with markers of a different color.

Facilitation

Ask participants to reflect on each of the questions and to record their ideas individually. Encourage them not to censor their ideas but to record all thoughts. Divide participants into four groups. Assign one question (and its corresponding easel paper) to each group. Before the groups move to their wall charts, explain that this activity is to be done in silence. Members of each small group are to "listen" to one another by reading what the other group members write on the wall chart.

As they gather at their assigned wall charts, one person in each group is to begin by writing a thought on a line coming out from the center of the page. Others add their thoughts to the visual. If the ideas are new, they will be written on new spokes emanating from the center. If the ideas are related to a previously recorded thought, they will be shown as branches coming off the previous idea. Encourage participants to draw symbols, as well, to create thought pictures on the mind map.

If you began with more than one question, ask each group to move to another chart and add their thoughts to it. If members of a group use same-colored markers, the original group can see where ideas have been added.

12. Interview or Conference

Purpose

Helps to surface issues and provide better understanding of deep—and perhaps unspoken—concerns; particularly helpful when individuals are polarized or unable to candidly and openly discuss an issue.

Preparation

Identify a setting where all individuals will be comfortable; avoid having a table or desk between you and the person to be interviewed. Develop at least one open-ended question with which to begin; create three or four others to pose as the conference proceeds. Consider using protocols or strategies to ensure honesty and understanding of one another.

Facilitation

Articulate the purpose, establish norms or ground rules, and help participants understand that your purpose is to better understand individual points of view around *a particular issue.* Assure participants that you are interested in what they think and that there are no "right" answers. Explain that you will be taking notes for your own reference, and that the information shared will be held in confidence; that is, no response will ever be associated with an individual interviewee.

Pose the first question. Use Wait Times 1 and 2. Prompt to more fully understand; for example, "Can you give a specific example?" or "Can you say more about that?" or "Can you help me understand your thinking here?" Throughout the interview, use effective communication techniques—including eye contact, nodding, and other nonverbal signals to demonstrate listening and to encourage reflective thought—and use strategies to help ensure clarity of understanding, such as rephrasing: "Do I understand you to say . . . ?"

Continue to pose the other questions at a comfortable rate. Refrain from giving your own point of view. During the course of an interview, do not discuss others' responses.

13. Interview Design

Purpose

Engages all group members in asking and answering a set of questions in a one-on-one setting; participants both gather and synthesize information and perceptions from group members in a manner that ensures that everyone has an equal voice.

Preparation

Prepare four questions of equal complexity around the topic of interest. Label the questions A through D and put them on a handout for all participants. In addition, create a handout with each question written on the top; make enough copies so that a fourth of the group will get question A, a fourth will get question B, and so on. Arrange the room so that there are several sets of eight chairs (a row of four facing a row of four), with enough chairs for all participants.

Facilitation

The Interview Design process encompasses two phases:

Phase 1: The Interviews. After participants are seated, review the process of interviewing. Ask with interest in the response; record what is said; probe, as necessary, to get behind thinking and reasoning; and refrain from making evaluative comments. In each row of four chairs, assign each participant one of the four questions, A–D; assign each person's partner (the person in the facing chair) the same question, so that question A faces A, B faces B, and so forth. (To simplify the process, you might want to place the appropriate questions underneath the chairs, face down, before the participants arrive. If you do this, tell the group not to retrieve the papers until they are directed to do so.)

Allow a few minutes for the partners to ask and answer their assigned question. Then, within each set of eight, have one row of four participants remain seated while those in the facing row move in the following order: The person on one end of the moving row gets up and walks to the other end of the row, and the others in his row each move down one seat to let him sit in the end chair. Allow time for the new partners to ask one another their questions, and then have those in the moving row move again. Continue this pattern until every person in each row has answered all four questions—and has asked his or her question to each of the people in the facing row.

Phase 2: Summarizing Data. Bring people together who asked the same question and have them work together to summarize the data they have collected. Ask each group to use easel paper and markers to record the major ideas. When all groups are finished, ask each group to share its results with the large group.

Tips

1. Provide context for each question by prefacing it with a statement or a provocative quote.

2. Use a timer and call time so that each person has the opportunity to pose a question and respond before the group moves.

3. Make accommodations, when the size of the group isn't evenly divisible by the number of questions, by adding a person to either end of one of the nonmoving rows.

14. Peoplegraph

Purpose

Engages participants in active thinking about an issue that is central to a planned discussion prior to opening the actual discussion.

Preparation

Formulate a statement that is central to a key issue in an upcoming discussion. The statement should be one that is likely to promote divergent points of view. Prepare a handout with the statement and space for participants to write in response.

Facilitation

Ask participants to think about the statement, taking time to clarify their thinking by writing individually. After a few minutes, ask them to decide the extent to which they agree or disagree with the statement and to be prepared to offer reasons for their positions on the issue.

Establish a continuum—an imaginary or real line in the meeting room or hallway—with one end designated "strongly agree" and the opposite end designated "strongly disagree." Ask each person to stand at the point along the continuum that represents his or her current point of view on the statement. When participants have taken a position, tell them to form a group with two or three others who are standing nearby. Ask participants to share with others in their groups their reasons for selecting the position they took along the Peoplegraph. After about 5 minutes, ask a spokesperson from one of the groups to offer reasons to support that group's position. Open the floor for comments from other groups.

Variations

This is a good strategy to use prior to a fishbowl, where the discussion can move into dialogue, with participants using active listening and other communication strategies to understand others' points of view. Some facilitators like to group people with opposing views, having the "strongly disagree" end of the Peoplegraph get together with people from the "strongly agree" end to promote better understanding of opposing viewpoints.

15. Questioning Circle

Purpose

Encourages thinking about a reading in order to identify key ideas and formulate questions about them; facilitates listening to and learning from different points of view about a common reading; and helps participants come to a deeper understanding—and make personal meaning—of a written passage.

Preparation

Identify and distribute a common reading (an article or a chapter from a book on the issue under study). Prepare written directions for the process.

Facilitation

Organize participants into groups of four or five. Direct them to read the handout individually and identify three ideas that are interesting—ideas they would like to think about further. Tell participants to mark these passages as they read so that they can easily find them later. For each of these ideas, participants should craft an open-ended question. This should be a "true question" (one they truly wonder about), and it should call for responses that are above the level of recall or simple comprehension.

Each group should identify (1) a facilitator, who will make sure that the group stays on task and that everyone participates, and (2) a volunteer to go first in posing one of his or her questions from the reading. During this entire process, as one person is speaking, others in the group should be quiet as they listen or take notes. This is not a discussion; there should be no back-and-forth conversation.

The first volunteer in the group selects one of his or her ideas, directs the attention of the group to the place in the reading where it appears, and then poses the question. After some think time, the person to the right of the question asker begins to address the question. Note: This is not so much to "answer" the question as it is to think aloud about the question, with the question asker listening in. When the first person finishes talking, the others, in turn, have an opportunity to address the question posed by the first volunteer. Finally, after every member of the group has discussed the question, it returns to the original question poser, who then can think aloud about his or her own question. This concludes the first round.

In turn, each of the other group members introduces a topic and poses a question, listens as the question is addressed by all group members, and then speaks about it. After all members have had an opportunity to pose a question, the cycle is complete.

16. Reflective Questioning

Purpose

Helps professionals become intentional and skilled in the process of reflection, listening, and asking questions that stimulate reflection.

Preparation

Prepare two written prompts, paper on which participants can write reflections, and a description of the Reflective Questioning process, including the three participant roles (see below). Arrange participants into comfortably seated groups of three.

Facilitation

Give individuals time for individual reflection and writing in response to the two questions (8–10 minutes). Call time, and tell participants that over the next 30 minutes each triad will engage in three rounds of reflective questioning. During each round, each member will have a particular role to play—reflector (speaker), interviewer, or observer.

1. The reflector is to begin the process by sharing thoughts from his or her written reflection. Reflectors speak openly, attempting to go deeper in their thinking as they are talking. Reflectors interact with their interviewers, seeking to use interviewers' questions to take their thinking deeper.

2. The interviewer's job is to listen actively to the reflector and pose questions that will help the reflector think more deeply about the selected issue. Interviewers pose at least two kinds of questions: (1) clarifying questions designed to secure information that enables the interviewer to better understand the context and characteristics of the reflectors' issues and (2) probing questions intended to get behind the reflectors' thinking and facilitate deeper thinking on the part of the reflector.

3. The observer's role is to listen to the interchange between the reflector and the interviewer, taking notes about questions that seem to be particularly effective in triggering deeper thinking. Observers also watch the two discussants, looking for nonverbal behaviors (head nodding, eye contact, etc.) that support deeper reflection on the part of the reflector. The observers do not talk or otherwise enter into the conversation.

Allow sufficient time (6–8 minutes) for the first round, in which one reflector shares. At the end of the allocated time, ask observers to provide feedback to their partners. Allow 2 minutes or so for feedback. You may then want to ask for whole-group sharing from observers by posing this question: *What did the interviewer in your triad do that was particularly helpful to the reflector's thinking more deeply?*

Repeat this process for two more rounds, with each participant serving in each of the three roles.

At the conclusion of the third round, debrief the process with the whole group by posing the following questions and using quality questioning strategies, such as Wait Times 1 and 2 and probing, to engage individuals in responding.

1. What did your interviewer do to take your reflection to another level?

2. Talk about the importance of nonverbals in the questioning-responding process. What can we take away from this experience that we can use in our everyday conversations?

3. What challenges did you face when you assumed the interviewer role? How did you handle these challenges?

Tips

1. Formulate questions that are mutually supportive. For example, you might ask individuals to reflect first on what they did regarding a particular challenge or issue and then to think about why they decided or acted as they did. Or, you might ask individuals first to reflect on and write about a strength they have and, then, to think about how they use this strength in their work. If individuals have made connections in their initial reflections, they will be more likely to continue that connection making during the interview.

2. While triads are conversing, walk around the room to ensure that participants understand directions and are on task. This is particularly important during the first round of the process.

17. Say Something

Purpose

Helps learners process a reading; increases comprehension by allowing readers time to think through a passage by talking about it; and creates connections by having learners connect a reading passage with prior knowledge.

Preparation

Identify a short reading that is on a topic of interest and that might stimulate discussion and dialogue.

Facilitation

Direct participants into pairs; each individual needs a copy of the reading passage. Give instructions: "I'll ask you to read a short passage. As soon as you have finished, turn to your partner and 'say something' about what that passage means to you. Then listen as your partner 'says something' to you about the same passage. There are no right or wrong comments; you may ask a question, agree, or disagree with the reading." Assign the short passage. After participants have read and talked, call time. Give them another passage. Continue until the passage has been completed.

Tips

1. This activity works very well with a bulleted list of items. Ask participants to read two or three of the bulleted items and talk about them; then assign another two or three. Continue until they have read and discussed the entire list.

2. Alternatively, a series of four or five provocative quotes works well. Ask participants to read and say something about the first quote. Continue to call time and assign a new quote until they have read and discussed them all.

18. Thinkathon

Purpose

Engages learners for a variety of purposes: solving problems, generating ideas, and reacting to others' ideas.

Preparation

Formulate several open-ended questions related to the topic under consideration. Post each question on a piece of easel paper, and post the paper around the room. Place several flip chart markers near each station. Divide participants into teams (one team for each question).

Facilitation

Assign a team to each question. Direct teams to gather at the posted easel paper that displays their question, brainstorm their answers, and record ideas on the easel paper. After sufficient time, direct all teams to move to the next station, rotating clockwise. As teams approach a question that has previously been answered by another team, their job is to read through the answers, placing checkmarks next to those with which they agree and adding additional comments or responses. When the teams have rotated through all the stations, they return to their original question, read what others have added, and summarize the team's thinking about their assigned question.

Variation

After the team responds to the first question, they select a team member to stay behind and explain their thinking to visiting teams. This team member's job is to record comments and additional ideas.

19. Think–Pair–Share

Purpose

Provides time for individuals to clarify their own thoughts before participating in a large-group discussion; and helps individuals process information, making meaning and connecting it to prior knowledge, through talking and listening to a partner and then to the large group of participants.

Preparation

Decide on strategic times to use this process to engage participants in thinking about a topic (might be used before, during, or after a presentation); it is especially good to use prior to a large-group discussion. Decide how you will pair participants and create the prompt that will begin the discussion.

Facilitation

As implied by the title, this activity is carried out in three parts. Pose a question, and ask all participants to *think* about it—usually through writing to a prompt or a question. Then ask them to *pair* with another participant and share their ideas. Finally, when everyone has had time to think individually and talk about his or her ideas with a partner, the pairs *share* with the larger group.

20. Tuning Protocol

Purpose

Encourages intentional and deliberate reflection about a specific work process or product through a protocol of talking and listening, in turn, with colleagues. The process of thinking aloud moves the reflection to a deeper and more meaningful level; and the use of a protocol protects individuals and limits defensiveness as colleagues share ideas.

Preparation

Decide upon a focus for the group's work (e.g., aligning student work to state standards; improving reading comprehension; helping students understand an algebraic concept). Identify an individual or small group who will present. Help the presenters select appropriate samples of work to discuss and reflect on with the full group. Reserve a meeting space that includes a table or circular seating so that participants can see and talk to one another easily. A timer would also be helpful.

Facilitation

Review (or introduce) the steps of the process. Lead the group through the following five steps, announcing the amount of time to be allowed for each.

1. **Reflection:** Presenters share what they hoped to accomplish, what they did, and with what results. Listeners *take notes but do not talk.* Allow 10 to 15 minutes, depending on the complexity of the task.

2. **Question:** If the listeners have clarifying questions, they may ask them at this time. These are questions to seek more information— not to judge. Allow 3 to 5 minutes.

3. **Feedback:** Listeners provide positive ("warm") feedback about what they heard; then "cool" feedback that includes suggestions for improvement. During this time, the presenters *listen but do not talk.* Allow 10 to 15 minutes.

4. **Reflection:** The presenters reflect on what they have learned, both through their own reflection and from listeners' comments. Others *listen but do not talk.* Suggested time: 5 minutes.

5. **Debrief:** Finish the protocol with a discussion of how it went—what went well and what didn't; how participants might want to change the next protocol session; and what was learned. Suggested time: 5 to 10 minutes.

Adapted from Looking at Student Work protocols, www.lasw.org

Tip

This process increases in value with repetition. As groups become used to the process, there will be less need for a facilitator; however, initially, a facilitator can help a group follow the suggested protocol.

Resource C

The Quality Questioning Quotient (QQQ): A Self-Assessment

Think about each of the items below. Assess your leadership questioning skills by using the following scale:

1 = **Novice:** In this area, I need skill development and practice.

2 = **Proficient:** I have this skill but do not use it as consistently or intentionally as I would like.

3 = **Advanced:** I am consistent in doing this skillfully.

In the rating column to the right of each item, record the number that best matches your assessment. When you have finished, add your subtotal scores in each of the four dimensions of quality questioning to help select an area in which to focus your improvement efforts. Add all four subtotal scores together to determine your Quality Questioning Quotient (QQQ).

| Figure C.1 | The Quality Question Quotient (QQQ): A Self-Assessment |

Crafting Quality Questions	Rating
1. As I confront challenges and situations, I identify core issues and form essential questions to guide my inquiry and action.	
2. When crafting questions, I take time to clarify the purpose of my inquiry.	

(Continued)

Figure C.1 (Continued)

	Rating
3. I formulate questions in consideration of the audience I plan to engage and the type of process I will use to solicit responses (e.g., informal conversation, interview, dialogue, structured group process).	
4. In framing questions, I am clear about the type of information I am seeking and use appropriate stems.	
5. I am mindful of how the wording and syntax of questions affect my audience's understanding of what is being asked.	
QQQ Subtotal for Crafting Quality Questions	
Encouraging Engagement	**Rating**
6. I possess a wide repertoire of structured group process strategies and use these to promote equitable engagement for all members of my learning community.	
7. I ask questions with interest in respondent answers; that is, people know that I care about what they think.	
8. I use Wait Time 1 (a pause after the question), as appropriate, when posing questions.	
9. I listen skillfully in order to fully understand each person's response and to convey genuine interest in the respondent's answer.	
10. I possess habits of mind to support quality questioning, including curiosity, openness, and respect.	
QQQ Subtotal for Encouraging Engagement	
Facilitating Thinking	**Rating**
11. I understand and consistently use Wait Time 2 (pausing 3–5 seconds after a speaker's response before speaking again) in individual and group settings.	
12. I use prompts and probes to clarify and get behind thinking.	
13. As I craft questions, I formulate "expected" responses so that I can plan appropriate follow-up questions.	
14. I am skillful in encouraging and honoring diverse points of view.	
15. I am adept at using communication strategies (for example, paraphrasing and asking questions to clarify responses) that assist individuals in uncovering assumptions and stating them publicly.	
QQQ Subtotal for Facilitating Thinking	

Creating a Culture of Inquiry	Rating
16. I am authentic and honest as I ask and answer questions, intentionally seeking to model quality questioning day in and day out.	
17. I habitually invite and encourage questions from others in my learning community.	
18. I acknowledge and reinforce quality questions and quality questioning behaviors.	
19. I seek to make explicit the norms and values that support a culture of inquiry and collaborative learning for both students and adults in our organization.	
20. I set aside time and resources to provide training in quality questioning, and I support collaborative inquiry across our organization.	
QQQ Subtotal for Creating a Culture of Inquiry	
Subtotal for Crafting Quality Questions	_____
Subtotal for Encouraging Engagement	_____
Subtotal for Facilitating Thinking	_____
Subtotal for Creating a Culture of Inquiry	_____
Quality Questioning Quotient	_____

Scoring Key for Individual QQQ Elements

15	Exemplary
11–14	Excellent
6–10	Good
≤ 5	Lots of Practice Needed

Scoring Key for QQQ Total

60	Exemplary
50–59	Excellent
35–49	Good
≤ 34	Lots of Practice Needed

Note: See Chapter 2 for descriptions of the four elements of quality questioning included in the QQQ.

References

Adams, M. (2004). *Change your questions, change your life: 7 powerful tools for life and work.* San Francisco: Berrett-Koehler.

Barell, J. (2003). *Developing more curious minds.* Alexandria, VA: Association for Supervision and Curriculum Development.

Barth, R. S. (2001). *Learning by heart.* San Francisco: Jossey-Bass.

Block, P. (2003). *The answer to how is yes.* San Francisco: Berrett-Koehler.

Brown, J., & Isaacs, D. (2005). *The world café: Shaping our futures through conversations that matter.* San Francisco: Berrett-Koehler.

Covey, S. R. (1990). *The seven habits of highly effective people.* New York: Fireside.

Cox, J. (2008). *Googling God: Searching for a faith you can believe in.* Eugene, OR: Harvest House.

Darling-Hammond, L., & Sykes, G. (1999). *Teaching as the learning profession: Handbook of policy and practice.* San Francisco: Jossey-Bass.

De Pree, M. (1989). *Leadership is an art.* New York: Dell.

Dillon, J. T. (1988). *Questioning and teaching: A manual of practice.* New York: Teachers College Press.

Ellinor, L., & Gerard, G. (1998). *Dialogue: Rediscover the transforming power of conversation.* New York: John Wiley and Sons.

Evans, R. (1996). *The human side of school change: Reform, resistance, and the real-life problems of innovation.* San Francisco: Jossey-Bass.

Follett, M. P. (n.d.). *Wisdom quotes.* Retrieved September 14, 2009, from http://www.wisdomquotes.com.

Fullan, M. (2004). *Leading in a culture of change: Personal action guide and workbook.* San Francisco: Jossey-Bass.

Fullan, M. (2005). *Leadership sustainability: Systems thinkers in action.* Thousand Oaks, CA: Corwin.

Fullan, M. (2007). *The new meaning of educational change* (4th ed.). New York: Teachers College Press.

Johnson, D. P. (2005). *Sustaining change in schools: How to overcome differences and focus on quality.* Alexandria, VA: Association for Supervision and Curriculum Development.

Jones, M. G. (1990). Action zone theory, target students and science classroom interactions. *Journal of Research in Science Teaching, 27*(8), 651–660.

Kotter, J. P. (1996). *Leading change.* Boston: Harvard Business School Press.

Kouzes, J. M., & Posner, B. Z. (2002). *The leadership challenge* (3rd ed.). San Francisco: John Wiley & Sons.

Lambert, L. (2002). Leading the conversations. In L. Lambert et al. (Eds.), *The constructivist leader* (2nd ed., pp. 63–88). New York: Teachers College Press.

Lee, V. E., & Smith, J. B. (2001). *Restructure high schools for equity and excellence: What works.* New York: Teachers College Press.

Little, J. W. (1999). Organizing schools for teaching learning. In L. Darling-Hammond & G. Sykes (Eds.), *Teaching as the Learning Profession.* San Francisco: Jossey-Bass.

Loehr, J., & Schwartz, T. (2003). *The power of full engagement.* New York: Free Press.

Marquardt, M. (2005). *Leading with questions: How leaders find the right solutions by knowing what to ask.* San Francisco: Jossey-Bass.

Marzano, R. J. (2000). *Transforming classroom grading.* Alexandria, VA: Association for Supervision and Curriculum Development.

Marzano, R. J., Waters, T., & McNulty, B. A. (2005). *School leadership that works: From research to results.* Alexandria, VA: Association for Supervision and Curriculum Development.

McLaughlin, M. W., & Talbert, J. E. (2001). *Professional communities and the work of high school teaching.* Chicago: The University of Chicago Press.

Palmer, P., Perkins, D., Ritchhart, R., & Tishman, S. (n.d.). *Visible thinking.* Retrieved September 14, 2009, from http://www.pz.harvard.edu/vt/VisibleThinking_html_files/VisibleThinking1.html.

Perkins, D. (2003). *King Arthur's round table: How collaborative conversations create smart organizations.* Hoboken, NJ: John Wiley & Sons.

Postman, N. (1979). *Teaching as a conserving activity.* New York: Dell, Laurel Press.

Preuss, P. G. (2003). *School leader's guide to root cause analysis: Using data to dissolve problems.* Larchmont, NY: Eye on Education.

Reeves, D. B. (2006). *The learning leader: How to focus school improvement for better results.* Alexandria, VA: Association for Supervision and Curriculum Development.

Reina, D. S., & Reina, M. L. (2006). *Trust and betrayal in the workplace: Building effective relationships in your organization.* San Francisco: Berrett-Koehler.

Rogers, M. (2007). Bringing life to organizational change. In M. Wheatley (Ed.), *Finding our way: Leadership for an uncertain time* (pp. 83–99). San Francisco: Berrett-Koehler.

Rowe, M. B. (1986, January-February). Wait time: Slowing down may be a way of speeding up! *Journal of Teacher Education, 37*(1), 43–50.

Sadker, D., & Sadker, M. (1985). Is the OK classroom OK? *Phi Delta Kappan, 66*(5), 358–361.

Schmoker, M. (2006). *Results now: How we can achieve unprecedented improvements in teaching and learning.* Alexandria, VA: Association for Supervision and Curriculum Development.

Senge, P. (1990). *The fifth discipline: The art and practice of the learning organization.* New York: Doubleday.

Senge, P., Kleiner, A., Roberts, C., Ross, R., Roth, G., & Smith, B. (1999). *The dance of change: The challenges to sustaining momentum in learning organizations.* New York: Doubleday.

Senge, P., Kleiner, A., Roberts, C., Ross, R. B., & Smith, B. J. (1994). *The fifth discipline field book: Strategies and tools for building a learning organization.* New York: Doubleday.

Soder, R. (2001). *The language of leadership.* San Francisco: Jossey-Bass.

Strachan, D. (2007). *Making questions work: A guide to what and how to ask for facilitators, consultants, managers, coaches, and educators.* San Francisco: Jossey-Bass.

Tennyson, A. (2005–2009). Charge of the Light Brigade. *Poetry archive.* Retrieved September 14, 2009, from http://www.poetryarchive.org/poetryarchive/singlePoem.do?poemId=1570. (Original work published 1854)

Walsh, J. A., & Sattes, B. D. (2005). *Quality questioning: Research-based practice to engage every learner.* Thousand Oaks, CA: Corwin.

Weeks, D. (1992). *The eight essential steps to conflict resolution: Preserving relationships at work, at home, and in the community.* New York: G. P. Putnam's Sons.

Wheatley, M. (2007). *Finding our way: Leadership for an uncertain time.* San Francisco: Berrett-Koehler.

Wheatley, M. J. (2002). *Turning to one another: Simple conversations to restore hope to the future.* San Francisco: Berrett-Koehler.

Zimmerman, D. P. (2003). The linguistics of leadership. In L. Lambert (Ed.), *The constructivist leader* (pp. 89–111). New York: Teachers College Press.

Index